Melbourne Magpie

Raymond Machado

Invincible Publishers

First Print in India by Invincible Publishers

August 2018

+91 8668639989, raymondmachado@yahoo.com

Cover: Vikrant Mhatre, +91 9764711188

This book is a work of fiction. Names of persons, organizations, businesses, characters, incidents, places and events are fictional and a product of the imagination of the author. Any resemblance to actual events or places or persons, living or dead, is entirely coincidental. Any references to hotels, resorts, churches, places, businesses, locations and organisations, while real, are used in a way that is purely fictional, and have no resemblance to any existing organisation, location etc., and any use thereof is not intended to harm, disrespect, defame or derogate any third party.

The views and opinions expressed in this book are the author's own and the facts are as reported by him and the publishers are not in any way liable for the same.

Invincible Publishers

G 120, Sushant, Lok 3, Sector 57

Gurgaon-122003, Hariyana

t: +91 124 427 3677

w: www.invinciblepublishers.com

ISBN: 978-93-87328-96-9

Dedicated To

All Migrants Of The World On The Move

With Love and Gratitude

To all those who inspired me

To create this literary piece.

Prologue

Migration is inherent to living beings–be they birds, animals or humans! Human migration is the movement of people from one place to another, either voluntary or forced and for various reasons.

We know from human history that most conflicts among nations originated as a result of movements of peoples who occupied lands of neighbouring clans, communities and later nations.

Millions of people are being forced every year to migrate from one country to another in order to escape death or starvation, brought upon refugees and asylum seekers by wars and international terrorism.

Then there is migration of ill-fated people who have nothing left to survive on as a result of natural disasters such as earthquakes, tsunamis, droughts, storms, floods, and of late effects of climate change. Men, women and children are being smuggled (human trafficking) in great numbers from impoverished nations to more prosperous ones, for enormous profits.

All such migrations give rise to serious tensions within receiving countries. In many places migrants and members of the host communities are involved in widespread conflicts. This happens especially when the members of a particular society of the host country feel that their own rights and distinct identity are being threatened by the influx of migrants.

Man's quest for a better living standards and better economic opportunities has never ceased. Over hundreds of years there has always been voluntary migration of people taking place internationally to satiate this human need but at a slower pace and in a more systematic manner with proper approvals and safeguards.

There has always been steady emigration of highly qualified IT professionals, Doctors, Nurses, rich businessmen and upper middle-class people, technical trade holders, teachers and labourers from various states of India to more prosperous countries such as North Americas, Canada, Europe, the Middle-East and also eastward countries such as Australia and New Zealand (Oceania/Zealandia).

Along with emigrants belonging to various religious communities such as Hindus, Muslims, and Buddhists-Jains from India, there are also Christians from Maharashtra (Mumbai-Pune-Thane-Vasai) and states like Delhi, Kolkata, Goa, Karnataka, Kerala, Tamilnad and other Indian States. To their advantage, the Christian migrants have culturally and socially been influenced in their upbringing by colonial countries such as Portugal, Spain, England and The Netherlands over four centuries, till India became independent in 1947. They have also been influenced religiously by the Roman Catholic

Church, globally administered by the Pope in Vatican City State.

India being a multi-cultural, multi-religious, multi-ethnic, multi-lingual and multi-culinary country, influence of its divergent communities on foreign cultural and social life is always variable, depending on their numbers and concentration in various areas in host countries.

'Melbourne Magpie', portrays cultural integration of Indian emigrants to Australia where they dream of having a better standard of living and disciplined working conditions than at their point-of-origin. Nevertheless, it is always a struggle to merge into cultures of the host country, for ethnic lifestyles, religious practices and culinary tastes of immigrants do not easily draw a parallel.

The bird Magpie symbolizes black and white, two shades of human character – one secretive within oneself and the other to deal with the surrounding world.

1

"Why don't you answer that call Darling? Don't you know I am in the bath?" said Vijay irritatingly.

"You always need attendants around you. Why didn't you carry your mobile with you?" countered his wife Maria in the same tone.

Rushing out of the bath and simultaneously wiping his wet body, Vijay looked at the instrument and shouted ostensibly at Maria, "See, it was Sanju's call. We missed it."

Goddamit, these modern housewives got the zing of modern lifestyle for sure! Thirty years ago while working in the Gulf, we not only could not talk on the phone but had to wait for months on end for a letter from home. Without communication we just imagined from time to time what could have been happening back home. That was agonizing indeed! And now these people want to take a call while bathing! Vijay thought.

"Don't you worry Papa Mr. Vijay D'Souza, he'll call again. Is this the first time we've missed his call?" questioned Maria rhetorically.

"You always wait for Sanju's call. Why can't you call him once-in-a-while?" said Maria as Vijay rolled T-shirt over his head and straightened it over his hips.

"You know he has free-call-facility from his company, so why should we waste our money," said Vijay; adding, "we have been waiting for two years for 'THE CALL', but the fellas want to enjoy life before getting bogged down to child-making. What can we do?"

"Let them take their own time...whenever they wish. We are not going to die tomorrow," retorted Maria in her usual manner.

*****

Sanjay chose Australia for his Masters in IT. Like many other Indian students Sanjay too completed his studies – 'learning while earning'. He secured a handsome job in an IT MNC in Melbourne.

Three years later, when Sanjay visited his native village -Vasai- located on the outskirts of Mumbai metropolis along the Arabian Sea, his parents were overwhelmed with proposals for Sanjay from matchmakers and parents-relatives of prospective brides. Sanjay had a wide range of choice from Teachers, IT Professionals, Computer Engineers to Dentists having independent practice and even MDs.

Half of Sanjay's one month leave went in refusal to settle down so early in marriage because that would deprive him of his juvenile freedom, he thought. Perhaps he was confused or looking for a perfect match. But he wasn't aware of the fact that so far no one in the world has ever found a 'Perfect Match' in marriage!

Anyways, just a week before leaving, Sanjay clicked with his 'dream-girl'. Those eight days were very hectic for Sanjay, trying to maintain balance between his compatriots and future life-partner.

During his vacation of one month the following year, Sanjay had a turning point in his life as he and Nilufer married in the Catholic Church, followed by a destination wedding celebrations with 1500 guests.

Catholic weddings in Vasai–a Portuguese colony for 250 years, followed by British Rule for 150 years – even to this day are celebrated in great deliberate traditional manner.

Close relatives and friends attended three days' pre-nuptial traditions and merry-making for a couple of days afterwards. Sanjay and Nilufer were in haste to get rid from all the people, to enjoy their pre-booked Honeymoon Package in Maldives.

Parting is always sorrowful for the dear ones. But Sanjay and Nilufer managed to get through those formalities soon. They were back on the turf in Melbourne.

*****

While returning home from the airport after seeing Sanjay and Nilufer off, Maria did not utter a word till the driver crossed half the distance.

Awakened from his sweet slumber by a sudden jerk due to deep ditch on the road, Vijay saw Maria looking blank and said, "Are you sulking Maria that Sanju and Nilufer have left us so abruptly?"

"Yes Viju, I feel empty inside… So many sacrifices have gone into raising our children... We provided for their each and every need… They did not lack anything the way we did in our childhood… and now they have just flown away, like birds from the nest!" said Maria with pauses in depressed mood.

Vijay shifted a little closer to her and stoking her back wiped her tears with his kerchief and said, "Don't be silly Maria. Look, they have gone there for their better future prospects. And they are not alone. In recent years the number of Indian students studying in Australia is booming. After the US, Australia is the second most preferred international education destination for Indian students these days. In fact, the Fairfax Media reported that in January 2017 the number of Indian students studying in Australia had crossed 45,000–the fastest growing source for the Australian education sector," said Vijay underlining that Sanjay and Nilufer had taken the right decision.

"What makes you think they will be much better off there than here, Viju?

"That's very true Maria. I had read in the newspapers that Australian Federal Education Minister Simon Birmingham, leading a 120-strong education delegation in April this year with Prime Minister Malcolm Turnbull's first official visit to India, had said: "International education is now our third largest export sector generating more than $21 billion of economic activity in Australia, supporting many jobs and providing benefits to both Australian and international students," said Vijay to bolster his earlier statement.

"Ok, then let's not worry dear. We will put them into God's care and keep on praying for their safety and prosperity," said Maria in a resigned manner.

As she finished her sentence, the D'Souza's already reached home in Vasai.

11

"Look at this fellow, now he calls after two days," said Vijay while picking up the mobile handset.

"Hi Sanju, where have you been after your missed-call the other day?"

"Dad, last two days were very hectic for us at Angliss Hospital with some pathological tests for Nilu."

"What tests?"

"Errh…Dad… let Mom talk to Nilufer," said Sanjay shying away.

"What happened to my Sanju baba?" said Maria impatiently.

"It's me Mama…Nilu…Sanju is feeling shy to break the news to Papa. I have missed my periods Mama! We consulted a Gynic, who suggested a few tests," said Nilufer in one breath.

"Oh! That's a great news honey we have been waiting for. Let me break the news to Papa. Viju, Viju darling, where did he disappear in a second?" said Maria over-excitedly.

"Hol…hol… hold on Maria…what happened? You are bringing the whole ceiling down?" screamed Vijay.

"Soon you will be a Grandfather!"

"When is the delivery date?" asked Vijay

"No man, just beginning…perhaps only the first month is over," said Maria in a subdued tone.

"So, what's the hurry? Let them confirm it from the doctors. Or do you want to book a flight right away?"

With that sarcastic remark Maria grimaced at Vijay dejectedly… even *after 25 years into marriage this man will never stop picking on me from the wrong end*...Maria said to herself.

Although in India matters of birds-and-the-bees belong to both sexes, traditionally pregnancy and maternity exclusively belonged to the feminine gender. It was natural that Maria became apprehensive at the news of Nilufer's 'good news'.

Participation of husbands with maternity matters of their respective wives is catching up fast in Indian metros of late. In remote villages it is still a taboo, a distant dream for potential mothers, who have to follow age-old traditional medications and at times cultic rituals.

In time-honoured Indian culture procreation was an obligation rather than a divine act. Although relationship between husband and wife was overwhelmed with shame, the union still fructified abundantly due to lack of education and absence of entertainment devices, such as radio and television.

In the following months there was not a single day which went without Sanjay and Nilufer telephoning the D'Souza's, updating them about Nilufer's pregnancy related issues.

III

"Darling, I'm getting worried as the delivery date approaches. He has been kicking alright but last night he was shooting goal after goal... couldn't even get forty winks of sleep," Nilufer kept on complaining as Sanjay drove her to the Angliss Hospital at Albert Street for a monthly check-up.

"Yeah sweetheart, just one more month to go and you'll be relieved," said Sanjay.

"Actually we should have worked on your parents' visas much earlier," quipped Nilufer with her mouth half open.

"Certainly, but we could not decide on whether your parents would come fist or mine," said Sanjay while entering the hospital gate. "Honey, leave our parents alone. Let us worry about our baby coming out first,"... said Sanjay with a wink.

"Baby will come anyhow, but I should be alive thereafter!" said Nilufer desperately.

"Nilu darling, have a heart and take courage. If you yield to negative thoughts, you may not be able to face those difficult moments," said Sanjay. "Besides, we have our people from Vasai Community. The Fernandes's, the D'Silva's, the Machado's, the D'Mello's and who have you! They will come to help us whenever we need them," said Sanjay more assuredly.

"I know, I know… they all are waiting for your pistol shot to start the race and come here running! All are busy with their own chores my dear," said Nilufer.

Sanjay chose not to answer that point and pretended to be occupied with parking the car in the lot.

These women will never change…they reveal their essence whether at home or in a foreign land. When they arrive first in Australia anyone's help is always welcome, but as they get rooted and acquainted with one another a sense of one-upmanship surfaces. At community gatherings initially they are formally polite but soon bickering creeps in. Sanjay thought.

Nilufer snapped her thumb and middle finger in front of Sanjay to disturb his day-dreaming, and said: "Oh Mr. D'Souza, the lift has arrived and where are you wandering?"

*****

Whenever Sanjay confronted the cliché "To Be or Not To Be", an encapsulated flash-back automatically unfolded on the screen of his mind:

Career seeking professionals from Vasai Catholic Community migrated to various cities of Australia a few decades ago. However, in recent years numbers surged manifold. Singles became doubles and doubles fourfold, that built a sizable community in each major city.

With sufficient count the dispersed members got organized by using the platform of the Church or that of the local Community Centres. Families started celebrating birthdays, Parish Feasts and Anniversaries, culminating in staging Marathi Dramas, from time to time. These replicated Vasai's cultural ambience through which migrants felt proximity to the motherland almost ten thousand kilometres away.

When many brains come together, there are bound to be clashes of views, agreements and disagreements, followed by grudges and hostilities. Vasai folks, -forming a miniscule count of 2.15% of Australian population and 16% of immigrants, were no exception to this mind-set. A few of them though, followed the principle of forget and forgive or live and let live! Other than that external social life went on as usual.

*****

"You heard what the doctors said, Sanju?"

"So did you," retorted Sanjay.

"But you were the one telling me to take it easy. You men will never understand what women have to go through," said Nilufer scornfully.

"Ok, Ok, babe, let's hope for the best," said Sanjay in a toned down manner.

The Gynic said Nilufer may not complete full term of pregnancy. That's worrisome; now we have to take extraordinary precaution. At this time having some elders around would have been a plus. Perhaps this is an inevitable part of an overseas migration package, I guess! Sanjay thought.

*****

Sanjay and Nilufer were both IT Engineers working in Mumbai. They both did their Masters in the Tata Institute of Information Technology in the city and were batch-mates. Since both were from Vasai and belonged to some 140 thousand Catholic Community, called East Indians, spread across the Taluq, they were acquainted with each other's family backgrounds and also had some common friends and relatives.

Vasai -15 km long and 7 km wide green stretch along the western coast of Arabian Sea north of Mumbai, was predominantly a farming land. Schools and Colleges started by Catholic Missionaries kept literacy at the top. With advanced speciality and professional educational programs in nearby Mumbai metropolis, Vasai's young generation made the best of the opportunity.

Weddings in Vasai took place either on love-marriage, proposal or love-followed-by-proposal or proposal-followed-by-love basis. Sanjay and Nilufer had a brief romantic stint but soon settled down with a traditional East Indian wedding revelry, lasting almost a week.

By the end of the last century a trend had already been set by young professionals and entrepreneurs from Vasai migrating to Australia. On top of family approval, migrating young couples also enjoyed exceptional social respect.

Such a daring move, allured with golden opportunity and adventurous thrill, had its own drawbacks that only the immigrants endured. For the rest it was like God's magic-wand-wish-come-true. Having gone through the ordeal of Visa processing, medicals, financial guarantees, etc., Sanjay and Nilufer had finally landed in Melbourne.

*****

Nilufer was impatient to call her mother, Mrs. Triza D'Silva, as soon as Sanjay and she reached home:

"Hello… hello Mom, can you hear me? This is Nilu…"

"Yeah...yeah… what happened baby? Are you alright?" asked Mrs. D'Silva.

"Yes mom…but there seems to be a little problem… the fellow can't wait…it's getting very painful…" said Nilufer.

"What you mean can't wait…you still have one more month. What do the reports say?"

Seeing Sanjay enter from the garage door Nilufer said: "Wait, wait ma…Sanju is come. He'll give you the details."

"Mama, three days ago they had done Sonography on Nilu and from the results the doctors concluded that Nilu would deliver much before the date…" said Sanjay in a serious tone.

"Oh my baby…how are you going to cope? Good God please help my girl…I'll offer Novenas to Infant Jesus at Nasik Shrine. Please Dear Lord, help my daughter out…" Sanjay just kept on listening to his mother-in-law pleading to God through mobile phone.

"Yes Mama, we will take care of her. We have the D'Mello's and the Fernandes' for our support in case we need help. And more importantly we have Australian neighbours, Mr. & Mrs. Brown, who are extremely polite and always care for us like their own. Please do not worry, just pray to God…" said Sanjay assuredly. "My parents should be getting their Visas anytime now. I'll check the status with them right away…I'm putting the phone down now, Ma."

Sanjay shook his head from side to side and said with disappointment, “Couldn’t you wait to call mom? Now you have worried her and there is no way she can hop in here to help you right away. What have you achieved? … tell me.”

Nilufer sitting on a chair holding the base of her bump with the left hand and leaning on the dining table supporting her bent head with the right, said in a low voice, “I’m sorry Sanju darling, I didn’t mean to disturb Mom, but I’m terribly scared! What will happen to our baby and me? Can you check when your parents are coming…darling?”

IV

"Did you check with the Agent about our Visas, Viju... hardly a month left to go?" asked Maria. "Plus Nilu is not keeping too well, she may come early..."

"Oh shit, I forgot about it completely."

"Yeah...I know your priorities...you'll never do what I tell you to...a day will not pass without meeting your friends at the square...sitting in the bar over cans of beer...and chattering about irrelevant issues!" said nagging Maria in one breath.

"Ok...ok...now don't give me a sermon please," said Vijay while picking up the mobile.

"Hi Villas, any good news about our Visas?"

"Uncle, there's a small snag about your bank balance. But let me check with them personally at the Australian Consulate, I'm going there tomorrow." said the Agent quite hesitantly.

"Viju, the doorbell rang, attend the door," ordered Maria.

"Oh, sure…just a minute…" said Vijay as he went to open the main door.

"Hi Mr. & Mrs. Naronha, come…welcome…come in please…." said Vijay while directing Naronha's to the living room.

"Oh, good evening Mr. & Mrs. Naronha, how are you keeping?" greeted Maria. "How is your son and his family doing in Melbourne?"

"Good…good…they are all fine. Sabby called yesterday and said you will be visiting your son next month." said Mr. Naronha.

"My God, what a lovely place Australia is! You'll love it, I'm sure. All their cities are clean and neat…no garbage strewn around on city-roads like ours…timely transport service…no serpentine queues for anything anywhere… everything is plentiful and people are nice… they are systematic and everyone strictly observes the civic rules." said Mrs. Naronha rapidly.

Mr. Naronha boastfully said, "Everything is available there. Our Indian Baniyas have set up grocery shops in every city and town of Australia. At times, there we get better things than what we get here, and that too without adulteration or duplication."

"Except some of the homemade things like East Indian Bottle Masala, *Nevries*, Rice *Ladoos* …" interrupted Mrs. Naronha.

"Do not get stuck in Melbourne only. Make time to visit Brisbane and its Gold Coast; Sidney with it's spectacular Opera House and the Harbour Bridge. On the way back you may visit Australia's Capital City –Canberra- and have the pleasure of sitting in its Parliament House. On the West-coast you may visit Adelaide city and don't miss the German town of Hahndorf on the Hills. Once there, you'll certainly feel that you're actually in a century old German village." Mr. Naronha gave D'Souza's a quick itinerary for travel in Australia.

"Well, well, our Sanju will take care of all that... ... but we must get our Visas first," said Vijay with remorse.

"What?? You haven't got your Visas yet? My...my... you better work on it quick," said Mrs. Naronha as an alarm.

In order to cool the worrisome mood, Mr. D'Souza said: "There's still time. Visa gets approved even a few days before departure. But we may anticipate..." Mr. D'Souza applied emergency brakes to the sentence halfway as he saw Maria's big eyes popping out, indicating he should not divulge about Nilufer's predicament.

To change the topic Maria said with raised eyebrows, "I'm worried about the overweight of the check-in baggage. The whole Vasai seems to know we're going to our son's place in Melbourne. Everybody wants to send something or the other!"

"Don't you worry Mrs. D'Souza, we don't have anything much to give to Sabby, except a few medicines for Scarlet and a little amount of bottle Masala!" said Mrs. Naronha while bidding goodbye to the D'Souza's.

"Perhaps half a kilograms of roasted *Chana* (Grams) to the max...!" added Mr. Naronha.

V

"Didn't I request you to send me home for confinement? And you said 'No'," said Nilufer regrettably.

"Do you have any sense, Nilu? You know we need to register baby's birth at the local Council here, how can we do that from India?" said Sanjay irritably. "Many of our Vasaikars are here for support, plus my Mom and Dad will be here soon, so what's your worry?"

"Your parents haven't got the Visa and this fellow is kicking hell out of me! You men will never understand what women have to go through." said Nilufer.

"That's your biological function, don't we men do ours as well?" said Sanjay with a sense of parity. "Besides, I'm running around doing all the domestic chores, just to give you as much comfort as you need but you seem to dig out male rudiments!"

Taking cognizance of gravity of the situation Sanjay shifted his temperament and said: "This God-damned Visas...checking everyday for the past three weeks but no luck. Last night Dad said, 'We are ready with bags packed. As soon as we get the Visas stamped, I will change the flight at whatever the cost."

"What happened to your Vasaikars? Where are they... who, you said...would be ready to help us in our difficult times?"

"Whatever happens to me, I don't wish to see that Sylvia Fernandes' face here," said Nilufer hysterically. "She is always critical of my dresses and make-up whenever we meet after Sunday Mass or for Community functions."

"What's the matter with you, Darling? This is not the time for back-biting. None of them know what we are going through. I understand this is very trying time for you but I'm with you sweetheart." said Sanjay compassionately.

"Auch, my God! Sanju, please hold me, it's paining me badly, excruciating pain, auch...Jesus Christ...please... please...come to my rescue, Lord Jesus. Sanju... Jesus... Sanju..." groaned Nilufer alternatively.

It was just 4 in the afternoon. Being a weekday, Sanjay thought, none of the known people around Melbourne would be home. But he heard a clatter from his neighbour Mr. Keith Brown's lawn mowing activity.

Sanjay had experienced that unlike Europeans, the Australian neighbours were more humane and always ready to help those in need. He also knew Australians held Indians in high esteem and preferred them to some other Asian immigrants.

Sanjay sat next to Nilufer and held her in his bosom. He picked a couple of tissues from the box and wiped tears rolling down her cheeks. "Take courage Sweetie pie...I'm with you..." said Sanjay.

"Sanju…take me to the Hospital right away…I'm dying…"

Sanjay called the Maternity Section in Angliss Hospital.

"Hello, Ward B here...may I help you?" said the Head Nurse at the Maternity Ward.

"Sister, please connect me to Dr. Bartlett, this is emergency…hurry-up please…"

"Jusss-hol-on a sec…" said the Nurse and handed over the instrument to the doctor.

"Doc this is Mr. Sanjay D'Souza. Nilufer seems to be critical, she is groaning with excruciating pain," blabbered Sanjay excitedly.

"Can you check if the bag is broken?"

Sanjay checked with Nilufer and said: "No Doc."

"So, there's no need to rush, as per our records she still has a week to go."

"But she is in great agony…do something about it Doc, please. Can you please arrange to send an Ambulance immediately? We're at Springvale, just 30 minutes away," said Sanjay.

"No…no…you observe her for next one hour and report back," said the Gynaecologist.

Sanjay felt helpless and didn't know what to do in such situation, the first in his lifetime.

It struck Sanjay to take help of his good neighbour Mr. Keith Brown. He called him on his mobile, but there was no response, perhaps because of the clatter of the lawnmower. He finally went out and gestured him to stop the machine. With a broad smile he came towards the hedge and said: "Yeah my friend…may I 'elp'u?"

“My wife is not keeping well and needs to be taken to the hospital immediately, will you please oblige?”

“Oh…su’r…juss…gi’me a few min’ts...” said Mr. Brown in his Aussie accent.

Sanjay got more panicky than Nilufer and did not know what to do, except to reach the hospital immediately.

VI

"What the hell is going on, Mr. Villas? What happened to our Visas?" fired Vijay over the phone.

"What do you mean what happened, Mr. D'Souza? They have been mailed to you three days back. I called you several times but could not get through to you, you can't blame me, I have done my job," said Mr. Villas defensively.

"Oh yes, our network is down for several days now. This stupid Bharat Sanchar Nigam Limited (BSNL) network is perennially dead! I've heard they do it purposely in order to promote private sector service providers, obviously with some kick-backs. Anyway, I'll get the copies from the Internet Café, thanks Mr. Villas." said Vijay hurriedly.

Vijay got outlandishly excited and started to shout, "Maria…oh Maria, pack up the bags, we got the Visas!"

Vijay took hold of his Mobile and dialled the Jet Airline office number: "Hey Gabby, can you book us on tonight's flight to Melbourne, we got our Visas already."

"Let me check the flight uncle, can you hold on for a minute?" said Vijay's nephew, Gabriel from the other end.

"Yeah, sure, I can hold as long as I need to, Gabby."

My God and my Lord, please get us out of here soonest. Let the birth of our grandchild be smooth and safe.

"Uncle, we do have some seats open all through to Melbourne tonight, may I confirm them?"

"Yes…yes, go ahead and send them on my email, please. And listen Gabby, inform Sanjay immediately of our arrival time and to meet us at the Melbourne Airport," said Vijay confidently but panicky internally. The D'Souza's had just a few hours at their disposal to manage multiple tasks.

Gabriel would do anything to please uncle Vijay, for he had some other interests with his first cousin Sanjay.

Vijay had to get things organized immediately. Sweets, Chanas, Pickles, Papdams, various cereals and clothes to be carried to Melbourne, were scattered all over the living room. Most of them were tit-bits for Sanjay's household-effects, eatables and clothes. There were also a few parcels from parents of Vasaikars in Australia and some parcels were yet to arrive in three days time, the original date for D'Souza's departure. There lay an open bag wherein D'Souza's personal clothes were just strewn around. Certain pickles and sweets were temporarily kept in the fridge.

"Maria, we got the tickets for tonight…we have to hurry up and pack our bags," yelled Vijay

"What? Are you crazy? How can we leave tonight? Are we going to Daman or Australia? So many things to be done yet! Parcels are still to arrive. What will Naronha's and the D'Silva's think?...that we purposely gave them a wrong date!" said Maria in exasperation.

"Let them think whatever they wish but we must reach there soonest. My intuition prompts things don't seem to be normal. I couldn't even inform my sister Lizbeth about the change in timing," said Vijay firmly. "Call Judy immediately, she will help you out."

The transport guy reached D'Souza's gates sharp 4 pm. After five minutes he started to honk the horn, signalling his arrival. There was no sign of the D'Souza's so he barged in through the main door and said, "Mr. D'Souza, please hurry up. We may get delayed due to heavy traffic on the highway, or else you may miss the flight."

Daughter Judith and her husband Nicky Fernandes had come to help Mom and Dad do their packing. They kept their two year old daughter Olivia home with Nicky's mother, lest she meddled in frantic packing. The driver, a distant relative and regular passenger haulier between the airport and Vasai, helped them secure the bags with straps.

As Mr. D'Souza lifted a bag, Maria shouted, "Viju dear, you forgot to pray to Jesus and Our Lady for our safe journey. Nicky will say a small prayer."

Nicky, Judith and 4 years old baby Olivia were to follow the D'Souza's once there was a Good News about Nilufer's delivery. This way Nicky didn't have to absent himself from his office as well as not miss Olivia's Sr. Nursery sessions.

Finally the entourage got on Bombay-Ahmadabad Western Express Highway No. 8 to the airport...

"Vijay, did you check if the back door locks are in place?" inquired Maria.

"Yeah, yeah...don't you worry! Judy and Nicky are going to house-sit, then why you get nervous?" said Vijay. "And what is this Rosary in your hand for?"

"I'm praying to Mother Mary to take us safe to our son. She has always taken care of my family," muttered Maria.

Vijay just shook his head left and right in irritation. *These ladies will always supplicate for God's intervention only when in dire need.*

The driver was very apprehensive about traffic jam on NH-8 highway, especially at the Versova Bridge over the strategic Ghodbundar creek, where traffic flow was made one-way at half-an-hour's frequency. Flyers invariably started their journey well in advance, but one could never guess what was in store. Missing an International Flight implicated waste of time and money and above all... endless hassles.

Vijay was not very keen in devout practices but now at this difficult time he had realised its importance. He willingly joined Maria in reciting the Rosary. The driver put to use his expertise and maneuvred the vehicle to Shhatrapati Shivaji Airport at Sahar, barely in time for the flight.

VII

"Please don't cry my darling, Nilu. Hold on...take a deep breath...we'll be there in a minute. I'm praying to Infant Jesus, he'll take care of our baby...you'll be relieved soon," said Sanjay requesting Mr. Brown to hurry up slowly.

Sanjay had already informed the Ward that they were about to reach. Midwife and Nurse Aids were waiting with a stretcher at the hind entrance.

As Mr. Brown turned his Suburban into the Hospital's hind gate, Sanjay's phone rang.

"Sanju, I am waiting for you at the Airport, I'm already out of the Customs," said Vijay.

"Who?...Dad?...which Airport?

"What you mean which Airport? Melbourne...of course? Didn't Gabby phone you about our arrival?" said Mr. D'Souza anxiously.

Hearing Dad's voice, Sanjay almost fainted. He could not let loose Nilufer from his arms though, nor could he make sense of the situation he was in. His shirt became wet with profuse sweat. His body started to tremble. Mr. Brown stopped the vehicle. Nurses rushed forward and lifted Nilufer in the air and placed her carefully on the stretcher. Before Sanjay could gather himself, Nilufer was already taken in the labour room.

Mr. Brown held Sanjay's both arms and shook him awake. Earlier Sanjay had sent Mr. D'Souza a fresh Optus SIM card and instructed him to insert the same in his mobile handset after touching down at Melbourne airport. Sanjay gave Dad's mobile number to Mr. Brown and requested him to go to the airport and fetch his parents to the Hospital.

Nilufer was taken straight to the Emergency Room, vital signs were recorded and drip started. Dr. Bartlett came and checked her physical condition and advised immediate Sonography. The reports indicated that full grown foetus' umbilical cord was entangled around its neck and one more twist would choke it fatally.

Nilufer was immediately moved to the Labour Room. Dr. Bartlett called in other Gynic super-specialist colleagues who unanimously agreed not to go for C section but to induce natural birth as soon as possible. The Midwife gave Nilufer an inducement shot and punctured her bag. All this while, Nilufer kept on groaning with agonizing pain. Sanjay, as trained earlier, had sterilized himself, put on a sterilized set of clothes, gloves, a head-cap, a mask and waited on his beloved Nilufer to deliver their first baby-boy.

The Good Samaritan Aussie made the D'Souza's wait in the lounge downstairs and left.

"Oh my Sanjuuuuu... ...where are you...where have you come?... where is my Nilufer with the baby? ... what happened to her?...why have you come into this God-forsaken country?" cried Maria intermittently and uncontrollably, attracting attention of onlookers in the waiting area. None of them knew what was happening.

"Keep quiet Maria...don't make a show here. You are not in Vasai...please," said Vijay trying to contain her frenzy.

"Why did you send him for studies here Vijay...I have lost my Sanju...my darling son, forever," cried Maria with a subdued groan.

In the meantime Mr. D'Souza went to the Receptionist and inquired, "We have come for the delivery of our Daughter-in-Law, Mrs. Nilufer Sanjay D'Souza. We are just arriving from India. Can we see the baby or talk to my son Sanjay?" said Mr. D'Souza rather hesitantly.

"Le'me check the Daily Status Sheet," said the Receptionist and depressed keys on the keyboard. "She is in the Labour Room. I'll message the Ward Head though," she said.

Mr. D'Souza returned to Maria who was seated on the sofa and still sobbing. He gave Maria his handkerchief. She blew loudly to free her nose of mucus. Mr. D'Souza sat next to Maria and held her close to him. He tried to pacify her: "What *tamasha* (commotion) you made darling... ... have some sense of where you are and what you have come here for...don't remove our *izzat* (respect)."

Maria placed both her palms on her face and placing elbows on her knees bent forward a little and started to sob silently, from within.

The Doctors were discussing whether they should go for 'Vacuum' , 'Forceps' or 'Vaginal Cut'. The Head Nurse signalled Midwife from the glass window to come near the door. "Is it coming?...How long will it take? The husband needs to go down for five minutes," whispered the Nurse to the Midwife

Midwife said, "Easily one hour". Going back to the Table the Midwife thumb-signalled Sanjay to go out.

"What's it Sister?" asked Sanjay.

"You're required in the lobby downstairs; not more than ten minutes, please," she said abruptly.

Sanjay quickly undid labour-room paraphernalia and rushed downstairs. Had a look in the lobby but could not locate his parents easily. They were seated in a corner but dozing due to jetlag.

Sanjay approached them, tapped father's shoulder and said, "Hi Dad…how are you, when did you arrive?"

"Sanju dear…where are you?...and how is Nilufer?" with this talk Maria awoke from her twenty-winks. While struggling to rise from the sofa Maria spread her arms wide open and gave a big hug to Sanjay, crying out loudly…

"My Sanjuuuu…. where have you been my darling son? I have been dying to see you ever since you left home."

Sanjay soothed Mom with a few loving strokes on her back and separating her from the embrace said, "Mama… I've to rush up, Nilu is in her labour. I have asked Charlie to come and take you home. Be seated, he'll be here any time now."

"No…no…I want to see the baby first," said Maria.

"Mom, the baby is yet to come out. And after 18 hours' travel you have to refresh yourself first," said Sanjay. "Besides, you two being here is of no use at all. They will not let you in till much after the birth."

"Why Sanju? I want to see my grandchild first," said Maria adamantly.

"Here's Charlie already." Before Charles could wish and welcome the D'Souza's, Sanjay said, "Charlie, please take these keys, settle them at home and let them get refreshed and rest. I'll be in touch with you."

"Hi uncle and aunty, you must be tired after long journey. I'll take you home to freshen up and relax a little," said Charles as Sanjay had instructed him.

"No, no baba, I won't go anywhere without seeing Nilufer and the baby," said Maria stubbornly.

."Aunty, no one is allowed to enter the labour room, except the doctors, the staff and the husband," said Charles to convince Maria.

"In our place at least one lady is allowed to accompany in the Labour Room…" said Mr. D'Souza hopefully.

"I'm afraid you'll get to see them tonight! Let's go home first…" said Charles determinedly and lifted their bags to load in the boot of his car.

As Charles Saldanha, one of Sanjay's friends from a neighbouring parish in Vasai, drove out of Angliss Hospital Gate, he quickly gave references of who's who in his family in Vasai to indicate their far-flung but inevitable relationships.

Charles stopped the car at 504-Fulton Street, Clayton. He off-loaded the suitcases and settled Mr./Mrs. D'Souza in Sanjay's bungalow and left to his place of work.

As a bachelor or a family head in a foreign land, one needed to have a confidant, a hand in need, a company for weekends, a source of village news and also to welcome new arrivals and bid good-bye to departees from Australia. Whether it was moving to a new house, going to malls, attending Community functions or even gossip, a reliable close friend was a always a blessing. The tenure of such friendships invariably worked on reciprocal dependability. Sanjay and Charles made the best of their comradeship.

"Hi, Aunty...hope you had sound sleep. I had kept breakfast on the table, did you have it aunty?" inquired Charles over the phone.

"What breakfast...why would we have breakfast in the night? counter-questioned Maria.

"It's already morning in Australia, aunty. You'll be disoriented for sometime but soon you will get accustomed to the time difference. I'll take you to the hospital once you are ready, I'm almost there," said Charles.

"What man....don't you know where you have come? We're at Sanjay's place in Australia. Come on, have breakfast and get ready. Sanju called a while ago and he has called us to the hospital to see the baby," said Mr. D'Souza to Maria who was lazing in bed.

"Oh, I want to see my baby first, let's go immediately... forget that breakfast," said Maria as she saw Charles entering the house.

While going through various sections of the Maternity Ward, Charles frequently sprayed sanitizer on his palms and signalled D'Souza's to do the same.

Charles rang the bell of the Maternity Ward and the Nurse at the station opened the automatic door with a press of a button at her desk. The D'Souza's were amazed to see automation at every step they took. They had to pass through several basinets in the neonatal section before they could finally see their grandchild. Nilufer gave a welcome smile from her pale face to her parents-in-law and asked the Nurse to lift and show them the tiny little bundle.

Maria almost reached baby's cheeks to kiss but the Nurse obstructed her saying, "No kissing of neonatal allowed M'am."

"Mom, perhaps Nilufer will be discharged tomorrow, you have next three months to take care of her and the baby," said Sanjay.

Seeing Mummy's disappointed facial expressions, Nilufer carefully handed the baby to Maria.

"Oh my…my…so cute baby! Just like Dada…my Sanju beta. Isn't he Vijay…look…look at him?" said Maria.

"We have named him Ajay, Mom," said Sanjay interrupting his mother.

"When did you baptise him to call him Ajay?" she said with a surprised look.

"Mamma, we don't have to wait for Baptism, here they name the baby before being born," said Nilufer.

"Then why not before conception?" joked Vijay. But no one laughed at Vijay's out of place witty comment.

"We must thank God…for he has kept both Nilufer and the baby safe and sound," said Maria.

“Oh no, we had almost lost the baby Mom, but the doctors here intervened in time to save him. I’ll tell you the story once we arrive home,” said Sanjay.

VIII

"Sanju, if Nilufer is up, tell her to bring the baby out for bath," said Maria the next day morning.

"No mom…the Midwife or a Nurse will come to take care of it, you don't have to worry," said Sanjay.

"No…no…why we have to pay for nurse when I am here? It's my baby and I'll massage him with the baby oil I have brought from home," said Maria authoritatively.

Nilufer became apprehensive about mother-in-law's over zealousness and said loudly from her bedroom, "the Midwife called up and said she'll be here any moment now."

Nilufer had no sooner completed her sentence than there was a knock on the door. Sanjay, rushed to open the main door of the house.

"Hi, good morning Sister, come…come in, we were just waiting for you," said Sanjay as he opened the door.

"Hi Mr. D'Souza, how's the baby and Nilufer?" said the Midwife by rote. "Where is baby Ajay?"

"In the bedroom Sister," said Maria enthusiastically.

The Midwife took Sanjay and Nilufer into the bedroom and signalled Maria to keep out. Maria's face fell as if she was denied entry into the plane, despite having a valid ticket and a boarding pass.

The Midwife took almost an hour taking baby's weight, height, temperature and swabbing the baby clean and recording every vital sign of the two day's old infant. She instructed the first-time-parents with minute details, the why's and how's of baby-care routines.

Coming out of the bedroom, the Nurse filled her bag with weighing scale and files. Maria just kept on staring what was happening around. She would never come to terms with the way an infant was taken carc of.

"My next visit will be on the day after tomorrow. But I'm sure the Council nurse will drop in tomorrow. In the meantime just follow the instructions I have given you," said Dr. Midwife and walked towards the main door.

"Doctor, what will be Nilufer's diet for now?" asked Maria just like in Vasai.

"What you mean diet, she can eat whatever she wants to eat," said Dr. Midwife.

"Oh no...she cannot eat cold stuff and she must have hot chicken soup which is heaty, she cannot eat rice and potatoes at least for a couple of months," said Maria with her village expertise.

"We don't have heaty and non-heaty foods as such. All food is good for the lactating mother," said the Midwife very politely while closing the door.

"Mom, why are you proving your ignorance before these expert medical personnel? You are embarrassing us, don't you know that?" said Sanjay rather irritated.

Sanjay thought: *She's my Mom alright but at times she behaves like an illiterate maid. What impression will the Midwife have of her? Well I don't have to worry about the Midwife, Mom is my darling Mom after all!*

"If you don't want to listen to me now, don't come and tell me when baby takes ill. We follow Indian Ayurvedic medical system and nothing happens to the child or its mother. I have reared two of you excellently!" said Maria very firmly.

"Do you mean to say that children in the rest of the world which are not administered Ayurvedic medicines fall sick and do not grow up normally? Come on Mom... we're in the 21st century, don't get bogged down to traditional ways when science has advanced so much." argued Sanjay with a serious tone and led Nilufer to the bedroom.

"Hi, Sanjay we are coming to see the baby this evening, will it be alright?" asked Sabby Naronha over the phone.

"Yeah...yeah Sabby...Mom was saying your parents visited them and were supposed to give some bottle masala or something. Come over and talk to her." said Sanjay.

"No...no...we're coming to visit Nilufer and the baby," said Sabby indicating the actual intention of the visit.

Families from Vasai Community paid courtesy visits to Nilufer and the baby over following weekends, of course with prior information. Some of them brought gifts such as toys, stuffed animals and also some gadgets useful for child's growth. The Gonsalves, the Machado, the Fernandes and the Saldanah paid visits to the D'Souza's one after another.

On one such Saturday evening, Nilufer saw through the wall-size huge glass pane of the house façade, Naronha's entering the gate. She called out for Sanjay, "They are here Sanju and daughter too."

"Ok, Nilu…I'll get the door," said Sanjay.

"Congratulations Sanjay and Nilufer," greeted Sabby and Scarlet almost in unison. "We can't wait to see the new-born babe."

"Nilu, the baby is sleeping, no? Don't disturb him now," warned Maria.

Sanjay ignored Mom's warning and signalled Nilufer to bring the baby out.

"Wow…marvellous…he's-jus-lik-an angel. Jus-two-wics-an-c-he-s already gone so tall," said Scarlet in an Australian accent.

Maria looked at Scarlet with a weird stare. And at the same time Vijay directed a very hard gaze at Maria.

Sabby's two years little girl Bella carried a package and handed it over to Nilufer. While taking the bag from her reluctantly she said, "Why simply you had to bring any gift?"

"It's alright, they are just a few baby dresses," said Sabby.

Mr. D'Souza requested the Naronha's to be seated and asked if they would like to have some refreshments.

"No…no…thank you uncle, very kind of you. But we have to go shopping," said Scarlet to avoid any more embarrassment.

Mrs. D'Souza appeared to be happy that the Naronha's did not wait for long.

Sabby walked them to the gate to bid good-bye. While returning he thought of counselling Mom about her conduct.

"Mom, if you don't know etiquette being followed here, why do you poke your nose into matters beyond your purview?" said Sanjay with a resolute voice. "People here behave with endurance and dignity, Mom."

Shaking his head in disgust Sanjay thought: *She will never improve…even after telling her so often!*

For the next two weeks Midwife or a Nurse from the local Council's Health Services visited the D'Souza's every other day to solve issues of the mother and child and to record its progress.

Hardly a day passed after Naronha's visit and baby Ajay became restless during the night. Sanjay and Nilufer spent sleepless nights. Maria heard the baby crying but preferred not to pass any comments. The next day the baby vomited the breast feed. It continued to do the same in the following days and cried incessantly. This was enough indication for Maria to conclude that as per village customs someone had 'cast an evil eye' on the infant. She put to work her traditional solution that would bring comfort to the child as well as Sanjay and Nilufer.

"Sanju baba…I see you two have not slept for several nights now. I think someone has done something to my grandchild. We must get rid of the thing," said Maria with tears in her eyes.

"What 'thing' you're talking about, Mom?" retorted Sanjay.

"I'm sure it is '*drista*', murmured Maria hesitatingly.

"What is that *drista* mummy? said Nilufer upping her eyebrows.

"It is casting of an evil eye on someone with bad intention," said Maria. "I know who it could be..."

"Mom why are you so narrow-minded? Don't be so doubtful and traditional, those days have gone," said Sanjay.

"Arey Sanju...this is nothing, mom performed this *Jadu* (magic) of hers even on our Labrador when he had stopped eating for some time," ridiculed Vijay with a suppressed giggle.

"You all can poke fun at me, but you'll see the change right now. Sanju, give me one dried red chilli, some mustard seeds and salt. Can you get me some burning coal in a container, Sanju?"

"Mom this is not our house in Vasai. We don't cook on *Chula* (hearth) with firewood," said Sanjay with rumples on his forehead.

"Ok then, I'll manage with the hot pan," said Maria and went to the kitchen.

After heating the pan she called out for Sanjay to bring the baby close to the kitchen entrance. As she tossed the three ingredients over the heated pan, a pungent smoke sizzled out. Maria made a few quick clockwise circles with her hand in front of the baby, taking baby's name she murmured a few undecipherable phrases and pretended to spit on the pan. The ritual was over. The 'evil eye' was supposed have been driven out! Maria gave a very broad smile that predicted everything with the baby would be normal.

By sheer luck or by co-incidence, everyone in the family was amazed to see the baby feeding, bubbling with smiles and very healthy in the following days.

IX

'The Australian Expedition' Act I – 'The Birth' unfolded towards its sober end with a lull at Sanjay's house. After the initial excitement of the arrival of the baby and new experiences of the first-time parents, things for Sanjay and Nilufer which initially were nightmarish were turning into a routine.

Maria kept busy with her self-declared, out of the script but glorified role; while Vijay had nothing to do after he watched international and Indian news on Television. Sanjay had purchased special package of Indian TV channels for parents' entertainment, especially the mother, who was very fond of watching Marathi and Hindi serials wherein Indian mothers-in-law and daughters-in-law always fought for supremacy in the long-cherished Indian joint family culture.

As the D'Souza's first month of stay drew close to completion, it was time to prepare for Act II – 'The Baptism'. Arrival of daughter Judith, Nicky and little Olivia for a month's stay was going to be a happy reunion of the D'Souza Family in Australia. And Ajay's Baptism function was going to be the climax. It was going to be an occasion for Vasaikars in and around Melbourne City to once again get together and enjoy the celebrations. Relatives and friends from Adelaide and Sydney were expected. Sanjay and Nilufer had made up a list of invitees. Other arrangements such as hiring of the hall, decorations, DJ, catering and the Compere had already been done. Nilufer had to just work on the Return Gifts.

Soon after flying from Mumbai, Vijay had taken a temporary holiday from his strict-diet. He had let loose his appetite for variety of Australian and international brands of cheeses and chocolates. Barbequed lamp chops and pork spare-ribs became regular weekend extravaganza. Such lavish delicacy deposits started to show on Vijay's waistline. Maria taunted Vijay from time to time that he needed to alter his trousers. In this place of ready-made clothing, marketplace-tailors like in Indian towns and villages were almost non-existent.

The only alternative left with Vijay was to exercise in Sanjay's backyard and go for walks in the vicinity.

"Sanju…I'm feeling little heavy and stuffy in here… planning to for an evening walk. Have any jogging track close-by? asked Vijay somewhat hesitantly.

"Oh sure…we do have Princes Highway Reserve Park in the vicinity. I'll take you there this evening," responded Sanjay with enthusiasm.

"But I did not bring my sneakers, Sanju. Can I borrow your used pair?"

"Why used ones Dad?...I will buy you a new pair of sneakers and socks too. Let's go to a shoe-mart in the evening. We have huge chain of international brands of stores and malls such as Wools-Worth, Costco, BigW, Myers and K-mart, " said Sanjay.

In K-Mart they sell great range of clothing, household articles, sports-wears, toys, home entertainment and all sorts of personal effects.

"Wow! What a huge store, as big as a football field!" exclaimed Vijay as Sanjay took Dad into the K-Mart at Brandon Park. Once inside, Sanjay took Dad in various sections of the Mart. An hour flew by without realizing. Vijay not only chose Nike sneakers but picked up many other useful items.

On their way back home Sanjay took Dad to the Princess Highway Reserve Park. The park had a full size cricket ground and jogging/walking tracks on its periphery. Near the entrance gate there was an administrative building and next to it was a community centre with indoor games and a library. Outdoors there was a basketball board, exercise stands with pull-downs-n-push-ups with exercise bicycles attached, plus hurdles stand and basket swing for children. Huge Gum and Eucalyptus trees surrounded the Park.

The Park was about half an hour's walk from Sanjay's residence.

"Dad, whenever you go for a walk please follow the directions I have given you last evening; and carry your mobile at all times. If you get lost on the way, just call and give me your location. I will be there to fetch you," alarmed Sanjay as he was readying to go to work the next day morning.

"Maria, how do I look in my new walking shorts and Nike sneakers? Give me two weeks, I'll reduce at least five kilos." said Vijay with puffed-up chest as he got ready to go for a walk in the evening.

"First reduce on your cheese and chocolates, in the meantime we'll order for a heavy-duty bathroom scale!" said Maria sarcastically.

With the initial enthusiasm Vijay took a brisk walk and reached the Park in 22 minutes. He panted heavily, so he sat on one of the table-cum-benches, sparsely placed in the area. He was watching children play on see-saw, slides and ropes.

Then all of a sudden there appeared on the table top a raven-like bird that looked exactly like an Indian crow. But this one had two colours – pitch black and contrastingly white patches on back of its head, extreme part of the wings and some end part of the tail. It had golden brown eyes and a solid wedge-shaped bill.

The ease, with which it landed on the table, indicated that the area belonged to the bird, that it must have been a resident of the natural open aviary of the Park and perchance its boss.

Twisting its head from right to left and tilting from top to bottom, it sort of welcomed Vijay to Melbourne city. It took a few steps further and pecked its beak on the rough wooden table top.

At home in India, Vijay would have shooed the crow away for their menacing scavenging ways, but he fell in love with this one at first sight! To him the creature seemed somewhat like human. It directly looked into the foreigner's eyes and almost stared at him. Instead of cawing loudly, it produced a hoarse rasping sound, perhaps meaning 'welcome to Melbourne, can I give you company?'!

A quick flash of St. Francis having a dialogue with birds in the gardens of Mount Assisi crossed Vijay's mind. But those birds shown in the holy pictures were of better class. Vijay looked around for the host crow's family members, but he saw none. Out at work perhaps!

Vijay couldn't wait to reach home and get info about this bird from Sanjay.

"Sanju, I saw a bird in the park, the same size and features like our crow, but it had two colours. What is it?"

"Dad it is basically an Australian Magpie from the Crow family of birds. They behave exactly like our Indian crows. They produce loud caws and grating coos, they produce a sub-song with rattles and clicks, just like the ones in India. The only difference is that in city habitat they are more clean and not detested. There is no chance of scavenging here, for no kitchen or animal waste is thrown out in the open like in India. Here the Magpies sustain on variety of fruits freely available on trees throughout the year. Occasionally though, they scavenge on dead animals in the wild."

That night the Magpie appeared to Vijay in a vision:

"Hi, how are you?" said the bird.

"Hey, you? I saw you at the Park this evening...on the table top," said Vijay in disbelief. "How come you can talk, birdie?"

"You're welcome to Australia. I want to be your friend while you are our guest."

"I don't need to befriend a bird. Let's be practical. Can you drive a car or carry my shopping bags?" said Vijay.

"Not that kind of a physical friend! I'll be your spiritual friend within you; like you have Guardian Angel in your Catholic religion. That sort of a friend, an inner voice, I mean."

"Well, be my guest!" said Vijay playing a host.

"No...no, you'll be my guest, I'll always accompany you wherever you go and whatsoever you do," said the Magpie, fluttered his wings and flew away.

Vijay religiously followed the exercise regime but there were no signs of weight loss. However, he enjoyed the routine for some other reasons.

*****

One day while exercising in the Princes Highway Reserve Park, all of a sudden there was a howling of a boy playing on an adjacent exercise stand.

“Mommy…Mommy Baba’s leg got stuck in the bicycle pedal. It doesn’t come out…” yelled a five year old girl to her mother.

Vijay was doing his push-ups on the next bench. Hearing the girl’s SOS, he rushed to the boy. After struggling for a while he managed to dislodge boy’s leg from entanglement.

The mother, seated on a garden bench fifty feet away, was busy chitchatting with an Indian lady. The girl dragged her five-year old limping brother to the mother.

“Oh my God, what happened to my sonny? No…no… don’t cry baba. Show me where you got hurt…” said the mother holding the boy close to her bosom.

As Vijay resumed his routine, the girl, thinking of Vijay as one of those Hindi film heroes, dared to approach him and asked “Uncle where are you from?’

“I’m from Mumbai,” said Vijay and asked “What’s your name?”

“Sarika.”

The girl rushed back to her mother and asked, “Mommy, uncle is from Mumbai, where is Mumbai?”

“Go and ask uncle,” said the mother.

“Uncle, where is Mumbai?

“Mumbai and Bombay is the same…but in Marathi,” explained Vijay.

“Oh, so you are from Bombay!” said the mother bending herself from behind the flower bush and making an eye contact with Vijay.

Wow, what a stunning blue-eyed beauty! a spark in Vijay's mind.

Vijay couldn't take his gaze away from that fair-complexioned perfectly featured diametrical sweet face.

"Yeah, actually Vasai is just about sixty kilometres from Bombay city. Where are you from?" asked Sanjay as reciprocal formality.

"From Bhavani in Punjab. But born and brought up in Bhandup, Bombay."

"So you too are a Bombayite then, good. What's your name?" asked Vijay.

"I'm Jasmine Singh, this is my daughter Sarika–six years and this mischievous fellow Surjit is four years," introduced Jasmine, while lovingly sifting her fingers through Surjit's hair.

"And what's their father doing?"

"He is doing his studies," she said.

Before Vijay could inquire anything more about husband, Jasmine hurriedly asked him, "How about your family?"

To that abrupt question, Vijay falteringly said, "Wife Maria and I are visiting our son Sanjay who is on PR and daughter Judith, married and having a daughter lives in Vasai. Like most Indian grandparents, we too have come to look after our grandchild, born just two weeks back."

"Oh, how sweet...but you don't look like a grandfather! What's your name?" asked Jasmine raising her eyebrows.

"Yeah...well, they call me Vijay, I'm Vijay D'Souza," Vijay acknowledged the compliment timidly and stated his name in the same breath. However, he didn't want to give up on her husband.

"What studies is he doing so late, Mrs..."

"Singh..." she completed Vijay's sentence and continued: "Here nothing's too late. The Company sends key personnel to acquaint with the latest technology, which in turn benefits them..."

"How long will you all be here?" Jasmine fired another quick question in succession.

Vijay guessed that Jasmine said it so quickly by rote, to avoid further inquiry about her hubby.

"Well, we have two years' Multiple Entry Visa with three months' stay at a time," said Vijay with hauteur to impress his affluence.

"Please feel free to visit our place; we live close by at 202, Ross Street, Clayton, you may bring *Bhabhi* (sister-in-law) along," said Jasmine.

"How long have you been in Australia? asked Vijay.

"15 years!"

"Do you work?"

"Oh, yeah sure... to make both ends meet I have to work," said Jasmine with dismal tone.

"Yeah...wouldn't be a bad idea to drop in one day. I'll talk to Maria," said Vijay as a formality.

"Mr. Vijay... please call and come, take my number 049876504"

Vijay thought that was too quick a wishful thinking on the lady's part and wished to get away from the precarious situation: "Mrs. Singh, I almost forgot…we're going to a Mall…I need to rush home...see you later sometime."

As Vijay started walking homeward, his mind stormed with impulsive thoughts:

This lady isn't arrogant about her stunning beauty... she has more Australian diction than Indian...she is so simple and unreserved...to a stranger like me she spoke so courteously without being introduced or without knowing each other from Adams. She must be starved for communication, companionship or love. I must be on my guards though...I always get petrified of beautiful women!

But she has invited me home with Maria...perhaps to repay the favour of helping her son or perhaps as a start-up. Should I tell this to Maria?...What will her reaction be?...Will she get mad at me?...Will she veto my evening walks?

I think I am going too deep...stupid me...got the habit of analysing and philosophising every damn thing! She could be genuinely generous and a socialite. That's why people call me suspicious! Yeah, but I don't think I am unreasonably a doubting Thomas...one must think of the opposites in order to arrive at a correct decision...most of my intuitions have wrought positively.

If she were born and brought up in Bombay, how doesn't she know that the city is also called Mumbai? Could she be feigning ignorance as a starting point for conversation?

With these wild thoughts and looking down on the walkway, Vijay had passed Sanjay's house a hundred feet farther. Turning back, he resolved to calm the mental tempest and decided to put the subject to rest for that night.

But the storm did not calm down. Rolling left and right on bed, Vijay tried to drive away the sprites but didn't succeed.

Next day morning, Vijay wished the clock hands rotated faster and evening came soonest.

Magpie: Why do you rash-judge people and draw conclusions? Perhaps she is emancipated socialite who wants to make the best of life. But if you want to play safe, take a break today. When you go to the park tomorrow, study her reaction to your absence today. That should partly reveal her disposition and from there you may pick-up...

"Vijay dear, you aren't dressed up for your evening walk yet, it's already passed your time. Aren't you feeling well?" remarked Maria.

"No, no, I'm alright...just a little headache," said Vijay while pretending to be attentive.

"If your walk is tiring you, give it a break, Vijay," said Maria with a concern.

"It's alright Maria, nothing more than a headache," assured Vijay.

"Don't worry Mom...I'll take Dad out with me to Coles... need to buy some groceries," said Sanjay, who had just returned from office.

Just over a month, and Vijay had already done a mental survey of Melbourne's demography. In the local bazaars and malls there were more Chinese, Indian and other nationals than original Australian whites. He hadn't come across any pure aboriginal he had read about. He also noticed many Australians married to Philipino females. The Chinese, over many generations, are well settled with businesses, trades and commerce throughout Australian cities.

"Hey Sanju...hold on. What's that crowd of Chinese people in the shop for," said Vijay.

"What shop are you talking about, Dad?" asked Sanjay.

"Tatts...what do they sell there?" asked Vijay pointing his finger.

"Oh, that's lottery shop Dad, they call it Lotto too. Some people always want to get rich faster without much effort. They believe that one day their luck will strike and make them Millionaires overnight," said Sanjay in a condescending manner.

"It's not a bad idea to try one's luck once in a while, Sanju," said Vijay casually.

"What! You mean you would buy a lottery ticket?" asked Sanjay with a big surprise.

"We hear the news some Indians winning huge amounts in Lotto in America and elsewhere. Out of millions of players, there have to be some winners...and one of the 'some' could be you or me," said Vijay as a matter of fact.

"People get addicted Dad...they don't win...lose everything and become pauper in no time," remarked Sanjay.

"I guess, retired persons who have no worries about career get a kick out of dreaming big and hoping against hope," said Vijay justifying his intention to play the game of chance.

On the way back Vijay got preoccupied with exploring another chance waiting in store for him at the Princes Highway Reserve Park!

XI

"Hi, are you from India?" said an unknown Indian person approaching from the opposite direction, as Vijay entered the Park.

"Yeah," said Vijay. "I am Vijay, from Mumbai... where are you from?

"I'm Bhupinder Singh from Haryana, came here six months ago. I've come on a PR Visa from India. I'm a Chemist by Profession and working for MNC – Nestle, as a Quality Control Inspector," said Bhupinder uninterruptedly.

"Are you working or have a business?" asked Bhupinder.

"No...no...I'm visiting my son. They just had their first baby...a boy. My wife and I have come for their assistance...in case...."

"Yeah...yeah...that's what Indian and other Asian grandparents do," said Bhupinder, interrupting Vijay.

"So, how do you find Australia, I mean Melbourne?" asked Bhupinder.

"Doesn't make any difference, because ours is a short stay of 90 days, plus we're globe-trotters," said Vijay with a feeling of superiority.

"Do you like it here or in India," Bhupinder touched upon the very crucial point to check with this veteran and confirm whether his decision to immigrate was right or wrong.

Vijay thought he should have asked the young man this question in the first place, because he had moved to a foreign land for the first time and that too on permanent basis. But Vijay's attention was divided. Not knowing from which direction exactly that dame Jasmine would appear or could be located, Vijay swiftly rotated his head intermittently left and right 180 degrees. But there was no sign of Jasmine.

"Do you have your family with you… or …a bachelor?" Vijay bowled a googly, knowing that many first-time arrivals get frustrated in short time due to homesickness.

"Yes sir, I have my wife Preeti, eight year old son Amarpreet and four year old daughter Jashleen with me here," said Bhupinder.

"Then what's your worry? Have some patience and things will work out alright for you by-and-by," said Vijay encouragingly.

"I don't feel comfortable here, sir,"

"Hold on…as time flies by you will make some friends," said Vijay hopefully.

"No need of friends, Sir…I have plenty of relatives from Punjab, Haryana and Delhi living here for more than seven to eight generations. It was upon my wife's uncle's insistence that we shifted here. Though I have a good job, I am not happy," said Bhupinder in a pathetic tone.

"There she's come with our kids," said Bhupinder pointing towards the Park gate.

For a fraction of a moment an electric current passed though Vijay thinking if Bhupinder was Jasmine's husband. But the moment Vijay compared her face to Jasmine's, he exhaled a sigh of relief.

"This is my wife Preeti and my kids," said Bhupinder as Preeti joined her hands and bowed her head in a *'Namaste'* to pay her respects to elderly Indian.

"Preeti, this uncle is from Mumbai, visiting his son. He has recently become a grandfather, does he look like one?" said Bhupinder in respect of the elder.

Bhupinder had formed a routine to walk down to the Princes Park from his Laboratory to spend some time with their children in the Park before going home. He indicated to Preeti to take the kids to play on slides and swings.

Bhupinder gesticulated Vijay to take a seat on the Garden bench. Vijay physically sat but was more anxious about Jasmine's '*Darshan*' (sight).

Why did she not show up at the PHR Park today? Could she have been upset because I did not show up yesterday? Was she expecting my call? If she had seen my 'miscall' and called me later when I was at home, what explanation would I have given to Maria? Perhaps Jasmine is totally unaware of what I am imagining! Could I be going through midlife crisis of my own?

"Sir, you have a wide international experience. Please advise if I should stay or return to India," said Bhupinder.

By this time Vijay had already construed that Bhupinder's was a case of 'Conflict of Class'.

"Which Company did you work for while in India and on which position?" asked Vijay.

"Sir, I worked for Britania India and held Managerial post in the Quality Control Department."

"And here you must be assisting someone not having more expertise than you, am I right," said Vijay slyly.

"Yes Sir, how did you guess that?"

"That's what is wrong with us Indians. That age-old class system has sank in our innermost soul so deep that it is very difficult to adjust elsewhere in the world, where there is no class or caste system. Here they treat any sort of work worthy of a person who does it. Whereas in India work is classified as per class or community of the person he or she comes from. We have learned from the times of British Raj to have peons and drivers in our offices, which means driver's son will eventually become a driver, peon's son will become a peon and a scavenger's son and daughter will become scavengers, collecting people's shit. But here a manager would get up to make photocopy of a document, make his own coffee or drive to any meeting himself or home after work."

Wiping the sweat droplets formed on his forehead, Vijay continued: "Back in India a Manager is treated with all pomp to buttress his 'false pride', but here toilet cleaner is elevated to a 'Sanitary Officer', because his or her work too is respected with equal dignity and it is very much an integral part and parcel of the establishment. Perhaps their salaries would be at par with officers and a cleaner here could be driving his Mercedes to work."

"Therefore, Bhupinderji, when you come out of India, you have to forget that discriminatory Indian system and integrate yourself into this kind of structure that bestows human respect to one and all. If you don't give up Indian traditions and come to terms with these down-to-earth practices, it will be difficult for you to continue," said Vijay in a counselling manner.

"Let me see, how it works out for some more time, Sir. If things don't work out good for me, I do have a very lucrative offer waiting for me in Bangaluru. That too is an MNC and they're paymasters," said Bhupinder with a wry smile.

"Alright, I have to work out a little bit on the bench... we'll see you around," giving this excuse, Vijay got up from his seat.

"Sure...sure...Sir," said Bhupinder and moved away to attend to his kids playing on the slides and see-saw with other children.

Maria was a stereotype and always maintained Vijay's timetable meticulously. Knowing that he would have to answer for the delay from evening walk, Vijay gave up on Mrs. Jasmine Singh for that day.

Listening to Bhupinder, Vijay remembered Indians who shout all the time while talking. Many of them do not know how to whisper, except while bribing a government official or while making love! In India people talk loudly in houses, on roads, in buses, as if applauding at a cricket match.

In local railway trains various ethnic groups sing *Bhajans* (religious hymns) while going to or coming from work. Thinking they intercede God's graces for all travellers, they go into trance and swing their bodies.

Many of these presumed pious people begin their day with prayers perhaps only to be excused for malpractices they would be doing in their business during the day. Other co-travellers lose peace of mind but cannot retaliate against the nuisance, for their religious sentiments are taken for granted. This is a clear case of exploiting and misusing protective shield of Secularism. Neither Railway Rules nor Railway Police Force can break the tradition, for the fear of igniting communal riots!

This can only happen in India!

XII

"Oh Dad finally you've come. I waited on you...we are supposed to fetch Judith and family from the Airport," said Sanjay as he drove out through the gate.

"I'm tired, Sanju. I think you better go...." said Vijay with fatigue.

Cutting him short Sanjay said, "Ok...ok...Dad...you better go and relax. I'll wake you up after we come."

"Maria, make me a hot cup of tea please," said Vijay as he sat on the couch.

"You look tired, what's wrong Viju?" asked Maria.

"Nothing darling, just want to relax a bit," said Vijay faking the turmoil going on in his psyche. That beautiful face, attractive mannerism and sparkle in Jasmine's almond shaped blue eyes had ignited Vijay's soul ablaze. All other senses had blunted and concentrated on amorous Aphrodite, the Greek Goddess of Love and Sexuality, an Indian equivalent to Rati, the Goddess of Passion and Lust.

Vijay could no sooner steal forty winks through the mesmerising spell, than there was in the porch chatter of voices and sound of bags being unloaded.

"Hi darling Papa, how have you been? We have been missing you my dear Papa," said Judith while entering the living room and extending her arms to give Vijay a hug.

As Vijay struggled to lift himself up from the soft sunken couch and hug Judy, Maria came out from the bedroom with the infant in her arms.

"Mama darling, (...ummah...ummah), how are you doing Mama?" said Judith while hugging and kissing Maria's both chicks. Nilufer also came out from the kitchen to welcome the Fernandes'.

"We are doing very well dear, but all the time worried about you and your travel with the baby. How was the flight? You all must be very tired. It's a long journey, no?" said Maria.

As baby Olivia entered the lounge room, followed by Nicky and Sanjay with bags, all of them exchanged greetings with hugs and kisses. Sanjay directed Nicky to their bedroom with the bags and said: "Mom, this bag goes to the kitchen; it has spices, pickles and other eatables."

"I will pray a special Rosary today for bringing our whole family together, safe and sound in Melbourne," said Maria.

"Yeah, now that Judy darling has come, you'd better got together and planned about the Baptism celebration," said Vijay with paternal anxiety.

"No worries Dad, Nilu and I have done much of the work," assured Sanjay.

"What work?...have you booked a hall...fixed the menu with the Caterer and what about the sound system?" said Vijay as a reminder.

"Don't you worry Daddy, Nilu and I will draw a list of invitees tomorrow and send invitations via SMS and Emails.

"Don't you invite any Tom, Dick and Harry! We must keep our distance from cunning people," said Maria while shaking the baby in her arms, trying to put it to sleep.

"I guess this arrow is aimed towards the Naronha's... that Scarlet," said Vijay sarcastically, elbowing Judith standing next to him.

"Mom...please...for God's sake...stop backbiting!" shouted Sanjay while putting his index finger on his lips and continued, "first of all we are a handful of people here and why do you want to bring Vasai politics in Melbourne?"

"So tell me, how was your customs at the airport? Did they open your bags?" asked Vijay looking at Nicky.

Before Nicky could answer, Sanjay interrupted and said, "They are soft on Indians these days, Dad. Provided you declare the contraband items and if the Inspectors are satisfied, they don't bother you."

"Yeah, but the Police dogs sniffed each and every bag of ours. Thank God they didn't tell us to open the bags," said Nicky in one go.

"I'm sure they had a soft corner for my Olly, she was fast asleep on my shoulders," said Judith taking the credit.

"Well, I've just put baby to sleep in the basinet. You all refresh and get ready...I'll set the dinner in no time," said Maria enthusiastically.

During the family dinner lots of news from Vasai was exchanged. But being jetlagged and fatigued, Nicky and Judith excused and went to bed early.

Australia being five-n-half hours before Indian time, Vijay parked himself on the couch to watch evening news from India. He was looking at the news but not watching it; he was hearing the narrator but not listening to him. He was floating in another terrain.

Magpie: Your attitude has gone bizarre lately. Does any sane person get afraid of beautiful people? You must appreciate the beauty of God's creation. You have to be concerned about people and yet be detached. Be a man!

"Hey Sanju, you've received Valentine cards already," said Judith in a teasing manner as she saw the cards on the coffee table, next day morning.

"Oh yeah...they are from my previous job office, sis. It falls on coming Tuesday and I have already done booking for 'family dinner' at the Steak House, downtown," said Sanjay.

"What family dinner? You mean all of us are going out?" said Maria with big eyes and raised eyebrows.

"Yeah Mom...what's wrong?" quipped Sanjay instantly.

"No...no...baby is barely a month old and even Nilufer cannot be exposed to outside weather right now!" said Maria sounding authentic.

"Mama, you're still living in old age. Gone are those traditions when new mothers could not step out of the house till after six months of delivery," said Nilufer in support of Sanjay. Completing her statement she said, "Now with modern medicine the mother starts walking within a day or two."

"Let's go and enjoy the steak Maria, when are we going to come here again?" said Vijay jokingly.

"Mama, I'm perfectly alright. Mothers here go to shopping malls with one week's baby," said Nilufer in defence.

"I don't know...I'll not be responsible if anything happens to my baby," declared Maria as a disclaimer.

"OK Mom, I'll take the blame if anything happens. As a matter of fact, sponsoring you all to come here includes all that," said Sanjay rather firmly. At this time Nilufer focused her eyes at Sanjay to take it easy.

Come Tuesday and Sanjay drove the family to the 'Steak House' restaurant where a table was reserved for six persons and a high chair for Olivia. Nilufer had learned from an office-mate how to put the baby into the Baby Carrier and handle it.

Sanjay led the entourage to the restaurant's dining hall and made them sit at the reserved table number 12. Judith seated baby Olivia on a high chair. As Sanjay signalled by nodding his head, a beautiful waitress came with a Menu Card with a broad smile and said: "Hi guys, welcome to the Steak House. May I take your order please?"

Sanjay reciprocated the greetings and said: "Just give us a few minutes please..."

"Dad this restaurant is famous for its steaks. People from surrounding area throng here for their sumptuous steak varieties," said Sanjay and handed over the menu card to Vijay.

Turning to the ladies, Sanjay said, "I don't think the ladies will savour beef steak, especially when it's rare. You may feel nauseating when you'll see blood oozing out of it. You won't like well-done too, because it will be tough to chew."

"Sanju darling, I think something in chicken will do for them," said Nilufer in order to save two guests from indecisive confusion.

"Ok, then we'll order for them – one Chicken Parmigiana with French Fries and Boiled Vegetables and another with Mash Potato with Salad. Will that be alright Mom and Judy?" asked Sanjay to confirm their order.

"Yeah, it will be more than enough. I'll feed some chicken to Oly from my plate," said Judith.

"And what's for you Nilu Darlu?"

"I'll just have Mushroom Soup as usual, Sanju," said Nilufer quickly.

"Ok, let's see what's Dad's choice," said Sanjay while turning to Vijay and Nicky.

"I would like a Medium T-Bone with Mash Potato and Green Salad," said Vijay.

"And for me a Medium Porter Steak with boiled veggies," said Nicky.

"Then for me a Rare Rump Steak with..." before Sanjay could complete his sentence and turn his head towards the counter, the pretty waitress was already beside him to take the order.

A waiter with a big jar of chilled 'Australian Bitter' came to table no.12.

Looking at him, Vijay said: "We haven't ordered any drinks yet."

"T'at's complen'tary sir, on the h'use," said the young waiter in an undecipherable Australian accent, which went 'supra caput' for Indian visitors.

Hearing the response from the waiter, Vijay had no choice but to keep his mouth shut, followed by Maria's big eyes at him.

The family had a hilarious conversation and ended with Chocolate Ice-cream for the ladies and cream-coffee for the gentlemen.

"Dad, what's your Valentine's gift for Mom this year?" asked Judith teasingly while playing with the ice-cream spoon between her teeth.

Seconding Judith, Nilufer said, "Yeah…yeah Daddy, today's the day…tomorrow it will be meaningless."

With that comment Maria tried to hide her blush.

"Valentine is for you young guys to celebrate! What would it mean to us after VRS? (Voluntary Retirement Scheme). I have always been a Valentine to Mom ever since we met, till now. You may ask her in my presence." With Vijay's remark Maria tried to hide a giggle by putting her palm on the mouth.

Though Vijay physically was with his own family enjoying Valentine's Dinner, there was a point in the centre of his being that refused to vanish against any stake.

*****

Sanjay's next stop was 'Destination Shopping'!

'Chadstone Shopping Centre' located at Malvern East, Melbourne, Victoria, is the biggest shopping centre in Australia and claims to be largest in the Southern

Hemisphere. It contains 530 stores spread over 1,29,924 sq.mt. floor space and 9300 free parking spaces. On its busiest trading days the centre gets about 68,000 visitors. On an average it attracts approximately 400,000 interstate and 200,000 overseas tourists a year. With 1.4 billion Dollars annual sales, the Chadstone Shopping Centre churns out topmost turnover of all Australian shopping centres.

The centre houses major anchor stores such as the Myer, David Jones, H&M, supermarkets such as Coles, Woolworths, Aldi plus Kmart and Target discount department stores, and jewellery/ornaments stores such as Swarovski and Michael Hill. The centre also houses Toys 'R' Us, JB Hi-Fi and more than 500 speciality stores which include high-end brands of fashion-related clothing. Two huge food courts satisfy visitors' international gastronomic requirements.

The visitors from Vasai were very impressed with the magnificent entrance to the 55 years old shopping centre, also colloquially called 'Chaddy'. Brightly illuminated main wing branched out to several wings and those arms also bifurcated into several other sub-divisions full of shops and hectic activity.

*****

Judith and Nilufer tuned well and wanted to enthuse the family-head for a bigger grab, so that their respective husbands would oblige in similar manner.

"Nilu, see that brightly shining Swarovski shop, let's see something for Mom there. Dad, come let's go into the left wing," said Judith.

"Oh yeah, look at our right, there's Michael Hill too... we'll have a better choice here," said Nilufer while winking at Judith.

Vijay, Maria, Sanjay and Nicky followed the females in a procession.

At the end of the day the D'Souza family members paraded through several internationally branded shops and added a few more Dollars to the Chadstone turnover.

During the youngsters' shopping spree, Vijay marked some shops which he thought might come useful for his private shopping some time later.

XIII

"Maria…oh Maria…where did you keep my sneakers," yelled Vijay, thinking that Maria was in the living room and would not hear him.

"Why are you shouting at the top of your voice when I am just behind you? And what speakers you're talking about?" retorted Maria in a similar pitch.

"Not speakers, m'a..am…my evening-walk shoes," said Vijay in a very soft tone, just to tease Maria.

"Oh, then say so…they must be in the patio. Last evening vacuuming of the house was done," explained Maria.

Vijay returned from the patio with shoes on, adjusting his black-and-white stripes T-shirt.

"Wow, you look young and smart with this jazzy T-shirt, Viju. Have a date?" remarked Maria with a wink.

"That's the one Sanju bought when we went to K-mart the other day. Why to keep it in the cupboard…for hatching?" said Vijay rather annoyingly and stepped out for his daily walk.

As Vijay closed-on to the PHR Park he spotted Jasmine sitting on the garden bench behind the flower bush. He pretended not to see her and went straight to the exercise stand for pull-ups. After about ten minutes Jasmine bent a little and waved her hand to attract Vijay's attention. Vijay saw the hand from the corner of his eyes but pretended not to have seen her, to indicate his serious intent in anything he did. After some time he walked towards the bench.

"Hi, how are you?...you're Jasmine! Where were you all these days?" said Vijay with a little bit of acting, it being their only the second encounter.

"Yeah Mr. Vijay...I've been coming here practically every day. But you did not turn up," said Jasmine very politely in a soft voice.

Vijay immediately sensed there was certain pain beyond those words. That hurt needed soothing words to comfort, a gentle touch on the shoulder to calm a troubled psyche, perhaps to mend a shattered heart!

"I did come but not at a stretch. My son Sanjay took us for shopping intermittently," said Vijay with an apologetic tone.

"Come...come...have a seat," said Jasmine while tapping her left hand on the wooden picnic table-cum-benches.

Vijay sat on the bench keeping a safe distance and asked: "How are the kids?"

"They are with my neighbour Karuna. She takes care of them when I go out."... ..."I was expecting your phone call for bringing Bhabhi to our place, Vijay,"

"She can't spare a moment...she is too busy with the baby. Handling an infant is not a joke. You've gone through it, Jasmine" said Vijay expecting a nod at least.

There was an abrupt silence...Jasmine's face turned serious...no one spoke for a while. But Vijay's mind was spinning:

I haven't told Maria that I have met this dame in the first place, let alone take her to Jasmine's place. She is bound to ask hundred questions, who's she? Where she's from? Is she very pretty? How you met her? Who started the conversation first? Again...even if I tell her the truth, she won't believe me!

In the mean time Jasmine went into a deep thought as to how handling infants is not a joke...

"May I ask you something?" said Vijay and continued as she nodded, "Tell me, what sort of a job you do?"

"Well, here the approved job visa does not necessarily and always match with the work you initially were selected for. If you don't have confirmed employment in hand, you have to take up whichever job you get, just to start your living in this new place..." said Jasmine.

"So, what about you?"

"Mine was a different case. I am a second generation citizen in Australia. My father came here years ago from Punjab. After a few years he got married in India and brought newly married bride here. I am the only daughter to my parents, but we have a few distant relatives spread around Australian cities."

"So, you did your schooling here, did you?" Vijay asked an obvious question.

"Yeah, of course where else would I go to study, Punjab?" said Jasmine with a witty smile.

"So, what's your husband doing?"

"I had told you the other day that he is working for a company and is out on a study tour," said Jasmine in a soft voice and humble manner.

"You also said the other day that you were here for the past 15 years and now you're saying that you are an Australian citizen," said Vijay to catch her lying.

"Oh yeah, I thought you were asking my cousin who was sitting next to me. She came here 15 years ago with her husband." Jasmine said in order to come out from earlier deliberate confusion, feigning to appear as an Indian.

With a small pause, she said, "After school graduation I did my Nursing Diploma. Initially I worked in a government hospital but I preferred to work in a local Safeway outlet, an international chain of stores." Wanting to change the topic Jasmine inquired, "How is the new-born?"

"Oh, it's just a bundle of joy...in fact a lump of flesh... God incarnate...a new human being out of union of two humans...inexplicable miracle!!" said Vijay while showing her baby's picture on mobile screen with his mouth partially open in awe.

"Wow, so beautiful and cutie baby. You're a proud grandfather now! Time to celebrate...bring Bhabhi over, we'll have a go..." said Jasmine.

"No...no...we're busy preparing for the Christening Ceremony to be conducted in the local Church. Religious obligations must be fulfilled before social ones."

"Yeah, we Punjabis too have Naming Ceremony of the infant. What kind of a religious ceremony you all have? What is that Christening?" asked Jasmine.

"While baptising the child he or she is brought into the Christian fold by performing certain religious rites in the Church. And after that we will have a dinner reception for our Community people living in the vicinity," said Vijay very plainly.

"I wish I had a chance to witness such a Christian Ceremony! I've seen infants in cute baptism gowns in pictures, but seeing the real thing in the Church could be an exceptional experience," said Jasmine.

"Yeah...Sanjay is making a final list of guests. The Church hall can accommodate only 150 persons, so he's cutting short on his office mates, he said," said Vijay taking a hint from Jasmine's smokescreen and put a full stop to her joining the programme.

"Oh, ok...I don't want to impose myself," said Jasmine in a humble manner.

What kind of a lady is this? No relation, no previous acquaintance and how come she behaves so familiar? As per Hindu belief could she be from our same bloodline in her previous birth? Why is she insisting on inviting Maria to her house, I wonder? Is she genuine or is it as a safety valve or just pretence? Such question crowded Vijay's mind.

*****

The Baptism took place at St. Peter's Church, Clayton, on Sunday, followed by a Dinner Party at the Church Hall.

The Compere gave a small introduction to the function underlining the meaning of Baptism in Catholic Latin Rite and Naming Ceremony. He also introduced Sanjay's best friend from Vasai living in Sydney who was chosen to be the Godfather and Nilufer's friend living in Melbourne who was chosen to be the Godmother. He then explained their responsibilities towards the child they were standing guardians for.

Over the backdrop on the stage hidden under a small curtain was the name of the Baby stuck in inflated golden plastic lettering. Godfather having raised a brief toast, upon count-down by the Compere, he and the Godmother pulled the strings attached to the curtain from both sides little by little to reveal infant's name to the guests. Simultaneously Sanjay and Nilufer cut the cake and Cliff Richard's 'Congratulations' synchronized with claps from the guests. The curtain slowly unveiled the name, 'Call Me AJAY' !

Everyone shouted in unison: "Wel...come...A...jay Wel...come... A...jay, and the Compere ended with: To The Human Fold."

As the function proceeded, the Compere called on the guests to dance to the tunes of long cherished Goldies and Oldies.

The female guests were served both red and white wine on the table, whereas, gents gathered around the Liquor Bar to choose their drinks from variety of Scotch whiskies or various Cocktails. Many Vasaikars relished and preferred hard alcohol to wines. The starters were served at the tables followed by five-course Dinner, including certain ethnic dishes with East Indian spices from Vasai.

Despite a special note on the invitation e-card which said "Your Presence is a Precious Gift to the Baby", some guests ignored it and did bring in baby-care gifts and soft toys.

Fully contented with the reunifying social event, families and friends one by one, bid adieus to the D'Souza's.

*****

"Oh...ah...uh...I'm dead tired Maria, can you please press my back a bit?" requested Vijay the next morning.

"Who told you to shift those tables and chairs?" said Maria with rebuke.

"I just gave a helping hand to the youngsters, because they had to finish the job before the programme began. We don't get casual labour in this place, don't you know that?"

"That was exertion enough to give you these aches and pains now," said Maria with disgruntle.

"But the show was great. Almost all invitees showed up and they appreciated the food very much. Especially the Lamb Curry *'Sukkha'* (dry) done in East Indian Masala from home," said Vijay as his mouth salivated.

"Yeah, many of the ladies too told me so, while parting," reciprocated Maria.

"Sanjay has a knack of organizing events."

"He's got it from you, of course..." quipped Maria.

"Yeah...the kids had frolicking time with balloons spread all over the hall at the end of the show," said Vijay in lowered voice.

"Mr. Albert was asking me if I could act in their forthcoming drama at Easter time," said Vijay.

“So what did you say?” asked Maria with inquisitiveness.

“I said, perhaps by then we’d have gone back to India. But what are you so excited about?” asked Vijay.

“No nothing, um…I have heard some stories about these drama plays,” said Maria with her lips open.

“What stories?”

“You know that Scarlet? Naronha’s daughter-in-law?”

“Yeah, so what about her?”

“There were rumours about her with D’Mello’s son Adrian.”

“What rumours?” asked Vijay with a wrinkled forehead.

“It seems they had a fling.” said Maria in a subdued voice, so that even the walls might not hear.

“Why are you worried about others’ lives, Maria? Such things are accidental and transient, nothing serious about it. Again that’s human nature and one shouldn’t make mountain out of a mole. Please, don’t take others’ worries on your shoulders, we have enough of ours,” said Vijay in a Counsellor’s voice.

“So, you approve of all that nonsense?” replied Maria promptly.

“I have noticed that in this foreign land also some narrow-minded people gossip and start rumours galore. They want to live out their Vasai culture with its vices to the fullest,” elucidated Vijay with his critique.

“No, but that can mess up one’s family life…the kids… the routine…everything goes haywire!” said Maria with a motherly concern and continued, “Therefore, I have warned Sanjay and Nilu not to involve in such cultural activities.”

"Leave them alone Maria, we are here just for a few months. These guys have to live without social life unlike us in Vasai. People in Vasai celebrate Weddings, Baptisms, First Holy Communions, Birthdays, Silver-Golden-Diamond Anniversaries, House Centenaries and now pet dog's birthdays too! Here these guys rarely have such events. So, if there are some goof–ups occasionally, we can turn a blind eye," said Vijay to convince Maria.

"Don't take it lightly Viju. It took a serious turn and that Naronha couple was on the verge of separation."

"When in Rome, you must do as the Roman do! So, immigrants in Australia are bound to get influenced by the host country's cultural characteristics. How foreigners coming to India easily fall in love with Indian Curries and also with our beautiful girls!"

"Whatever it may be, but I would not tolerate something like this happening to our Sanjay and Nilufer."

"Maria don't put all the apples in the same basket. We know our Sanjay well from the way we have brought him up," concluded Vijay abruptly.

XIV

After the Christening Ceremony, meetings between Vijay and Jasmine at the Princes Highway Reserve Park became quite frequent. By now the stiffness of mannerism had evaporated and both had come down to earth with few reservations.

"You know Vijay, I want to tell you something but don't know if you'll like it," said Jasmine with a little quivering voice.

"Oh, go ahead and say it, I'm a sport," said Vijay very lightly.

"Vijay, I don't know what's gone wrong with me, but these days I anxiously long for the evenings to arrive. I feel comfortable meeting and talking with you. When you don't show up, I find it difficult to even sleep, thinking what must have held you up. Then all sorts of thoughts storm my mind till weary eyes close automatically much after midnight." Jasmine looked down on the ground and then suddenly lifting her head and looking straight into Vijay's eyes, said: "Vijay I have started to miss you…!"

Instantly Vijay was bowled out and dumbfounded. With his mouth half open he looked into Jasmine's blue eyes. He was flabbergasted with that erotic statement. He did not know what to say or do at Jasmine's ludicrous comment. He was a Counsellor to the core and did not wish to react to Jasmine's feelings immediately. He thought she must be going through a rough patch with her husband or children or for any other personal reason.

"Jasmine, what's wrong with you today? You don't seem to be normal like any other day!" said Vijay with a worried face.

"I'm sorry Vijay, but please understand me. I feel lonely and scared. I'm fed-up of life...I don't want to live any more...Vijay... please understand me." Her eyes welled up...suddenly the pearly tears started to drop on her breasts. She could no more look into Vijay's eyes, for her vision became blurred. So she covered her face with her palms, leaned towards Vijay and rested her sobbing head on his shoulders.

"Now hold...hold on Jasmine...take it easy. What's the matter with you? Did you have a fight with your husband? Did he beat you up? What happened to you? Just say something. It's embarrassing to make a show in public place like this, Jasmine. See those Indian kids and ladies are looking at us," said Vijay with a serious tone.

Without saying a word, Jasmine just kept on sulking and shedding tears.

The night went tough for Vijay.

"Vijay...Viju...wake up, it's 9 O'clock already. The Sun is strong and soon it's going to pour out fire. C'mon darling, your breakfast has gone cold..." said Maria.

“Uh…um…I don’t have to catch Churchgate fast train any more. These are holidays…leave me alone Maria,” said Vijay and turned his back on Maria.

Practically the whole night Vijay’s head was spinning as if on a horizontal giant wheel. He couldn’t make sense of anything what Jasmine was going through. At this juncture he needed to have more conversations and question-answer sessions with her, in order to direct her on the right track.

Planning next day’s strategy had consumed his sleep. But all this was going to be without the knowledge of Maria and to a certain degree Sanjay and Nilufer too. Vijay always preferred to be open but knowing Maria’s over-protectively suspicious nature Vijay had to act prudently.

“Are you not going to the park today? It’s already five in the evening!” said Maria while wiping plates from the dishwasher.

“I don’t know…I’m not feeling too well today.” Said Vijay but soon decided to dress up for the walk.

Without realizing how fast he walked, Vijay found himself at the park and had already started his routine exercise. After a while he saw the dame entering park gates with her eyesight towards the ground. She quietly sat on the usual garden table-cum-bench, apparently in deep thoughts.

“Hi…how are you today?” said Vijay as Jasmine lifted her head to look up at Vijay. “Your eyes look sore.”

“And so are yours…much more than mine. Didn’t you sleep well last night?” asked Jasmine in a soft and loving manner.

That feeble and loving voice sent an electrifying vibration in Vijay's being.

"You see Jasmine, I am a Counsellor to troubled families in our town. People seek advice from me for youngsters having problems with parents or young married couples unable to adjust to newfound cohabitation. Unless and until I know your exact situation, I will not be able to guide you on the right path." said Vijay on a professional note.

"I feel embarrassed; I don't know where to begin."

"Is it your husband, mother, neighbour or a friend?"

Jasmine kept silent for a couple of minutes staring on the table top.

"Why don't you speak out…say something? Don't harbour any ill feelings within your heart for long. They have adverse effect on health."

"I want to share with you everything but I am ashamed of myself at the same time. It's very personal…" said Jasmine while her eyes closed.

"I don't mean to force you to tell me anything for that matter. But yesterday the way you broke down, there's something very serious which needs immediate attention," said Vijay with concern.

Jasmine remained quiet for a few minutes and lifting her head and looking up in the sky said: "He's come."

"Who he?"

"Jim."

"When?"

"A couple of days back."

"You didn't say a word about it yesterday?"

"I couldn't have...I don't want to think of him...he scares me...he is not human...he's a beast...a bastard!" said Jasmine pausing in between phrases.

"Look here Jasmine, we cannot discuss these things in a public place like this."

"I've been calling you to my house but you're ignoring it."

"Not that I'm ignoring, but Maria cannot leave the baby and come out with me on long social visits," excused Vijay.

"You could have come alone, if you wanted to," quipped Jasmine promptly.

"But what will people think of me coming to your house alone?"

"Which people?"

"Your neighbours?"

"To hang with the neighbours! Here no one bothers who comes to your house or who goes out," said Jasmine as a matter of fact.

"OK, I will try to come tomorrow. And perhaps I could talk to Jim as well," said Vijay while shaking his head.

"No...no; he's not in a good mood. He's going back to Canada tomorrow. We could meet the day after," said Jasmine.

"Is he on a Company job in Canada?"

"Yeah, I told you he is upgrading for a new project in Adelaide," said Jasmine with a little annoyance. "He has his sister living at the same area in Canada, so he couldn't be missing this place, I guess," she added.

"Oh...ok...it could be 'mid-life crisis."

"What is that?"

"I will explain it to you in our sessions," he said.

"Why are you rushing so fast Vijay. Wait on; I need some moral support, please."

"We're expecting some guests this evening and Maria warned me to come home soon," said Vijay while getting up from the garden bench.

"Ok, see you the day after tomorrow at the same time here. But I'll call you to confirm it... take care."

"You too...and take it easy with Jim. And remember, don't call me on my mobile. Max, you may send an SMS," said Vijay and left the park in hurry.

On his way back home Vijay would always review their conversation by each sentence to find if there was any sneaky move by the female. So far he had judged her innocent and victimised.

*****

Sports had played a very vital role in Vijay's uprightness. From his college-cum-boarding years Vijay was versatile in many a game, Basketball being his favourite. While playing he would follow the rules of the game very meticulously. A couple of good-heighted foreign professors would also participate and that brought a touch of seriousness to the practice sessions.

One among ten players would referee the game. A couple of times Vijay had taken objections to the referee's foul decisions and technically he was proved to be right. From that time he became the 'whistle-blower'.

Brother Tom had a flexible body. He would dodge opponents and dribble the ball from one end of the court straight to the basket. But Vijay, the Referee, would disallow that goal, though technically correct but not in tune with the sporting spirit. According to him, the other four players in the team were not spectators or would simply run back and forth without touching the ball! Thus Vijay had added the rule of 'no Solo' to their unwritten rule-book.

From that time Vijay saw to the needs of everyone with cooperation and contribution of all involved. He had mastered the art of authority in its proper sense with justice to all. Therefore, he did not have any qualms about dealing with any kind of person – be it in a high or low position, be it a male or a female, be it a mediocre or a beautiful one.

*****

On reaching home, Vijay realized that all were waiting for him to go for an 'evening out'.

"C'mon Dad, I'm sure you've forgotten as usual." said Sanjay shaking his head from side to side.

"What's up now? You all are dressed up, are we going somewhere?" said Vijay with a surprised expression. "Oh my little Ajay also is ready to go out," said Vijay while holding the baby and playing with it.

"I told you Sanju, papa is not present here these days. I don't know what's wrong with him. He has become very forgetful," commented Maria.

"Yeah...I'm always preoccupied with my writing... don't you know that? And that is the reason I brought my laptop here," said Vijay as a matter of fact.

"C'mon let's go now...our tables are reserved and we can't be late..."said Sanjay while taking the baby to the Car.

As Sanjay struggled to strap the tiny baby to the safety seat, Vijay remarked, "It is easier to make babies than to fix them to safety seats!"

This time Sanjay's destination was Pizza Hut at Springvale Road. Sanjay intended to take parents to maximum places during their limited stay as and when feasible. He preferred to take them out for dinner at food-courts in shopping complexes with the intention of buying tit-bits for them to take home.

Jasmine's charm, camouflaged under the garb of victimization, was working on Vijay with a snail's pace but for certain. She had her target fixed and also the *modus operandi*. Only time was a delaying factor but necessary for the process.

Vijay saw from far this slim bodied fair and blue-eyed woman taking slow strides on the walkway in front of the PHR Park gates. He wondered – why this beautiful young lady has to go through this ordeal. Why her husband couldn't understand and love her despite her shortcomings?

Magpie: Hey…hey…hold on buddy. It may be alright to empathise with the lady but once you start to sympathise with her, you may get emotionally hooked. Watch your move; you may get into deep shit…!

C'mon my scruple, I know it. This is not the first time I'm dealing with a troubled soul. Plus you are always within me to pull the reigns.

“Hi there,” she looked at her wrist watch and said: “You are dot on time.”

“Yeah, I don’t like to keep people waiting for me and vice versa. That way we give respect to each other and value for their time,” said Vijay while turning to enter the gates.

“Ah…ha…no Mr. Vijay, we’ve planned to visit my house today.”

“Oh yeah, sure; but I could do just half my daily routine before we proceed. Otherwise my body will starve.”

‘I won’t let it happen’, a spark crossed Jasmine’s mind!

The west-side mid-summer Sun was shining strong on Vijay as he did pull-ups. Jasmine kept on watching him sweat out. Sun’s amber shade reflected on Vijay’s face like a hero in a Country Western Cowboy Hollywood movie, she imagined.

Vijay did some speed-cycling and panting heavily came towards Jasmine. Regular visitors had got used to Vijay and Jasmine sitting at any one of the picnic tables in the Park.

Seeing Vijay coming towards her, Jasmine stood up and said: “You must be feeling lighter now!” and started to walk out of the Park.

“So tell me something about yourself, Vijay. We hardly know each other and behave as if we were friends for ages.”

“Yeah, you’re right. I too was wondering how in a short span we have tuned well,” said Vijay in support of Jasmine’s opinion.

“How far is your house from here?”

"Just about ten minutes' walk…202, Ross Street"

"I hope I don't get lost while returning home since there are so many boulevards, circles, avenues, streets and roads. I'm new to the vicinity and they confuse me."

"Yeah, I understand. Worry not, I'll reach you back, in case…" said Jasmine with assurance.

"How are the kids? I forgot their names…"

"Sarika and Surjit…yeah, they're alright. But actually to tell you the truth Vijay, they are not mine!

"What? Then whose are they?"

"Remember you met my cousin Karuna on the first day at the Park? They are her's. I babysit them whenever she has important work outside. I love them so much and so they call me also mommy."

"Oh, you didn't say so at that time."

"At that time we were just taken up by your presence, plus you had helped Surjit with his leg stuck in the cycle pedal… didn't exactly know what to converse."

"So, your husband left for Canada yesterday?"

"Yeah, good riddance to the bad rubbish…" Jasmine said with firm voice.

"Why do you always talk negative about him?" asked Vijay.

"Because he doesn't do anything positive." she said.

"What you mean?"

"Vijay, this is very personal and not to be spoken out on the road like this." she said sternly. "We have already reached our place. Let's talk about it in the house."

Jasmine opened the main door and let Vijay in the living room. The furniture was heavy and occupied much space. The floor carpet was quite puffy.

"Jasmine, it's quite stuffy in here, can you start the AC please," requested Vijay.

"Oh…yeah…sure."

"Have a seat Vijay, feel at home, no one's here."

"No…no…I'm wet, so let my shirt dry a little."

Coming close and sniffing him, she said: "Your sweat smells like lavender with a hint of musk! I love it!!"

"You want to have a shower?" Coaxing Vijay towards the bathroom she said, "C'mon…just get in…turn the spindle to your left for hot water and to your right for cold. You start and I'll keep a fresh towel ready for you," said Jasmine like she would say to her own.

It was so quick, Vijay didn't have any time to reflect what he should do and what not at that moment. He got into the shower and closed the door behind him. He checked if it could open by applying force. It did not open, so he thought it had locked magnetically. Since sufficient sunlight was coming through one-way window pane, he did not put the lights on. He undressed and hung his clothes to the hooks on the wall. He was about to open the tap but suddenly Jasmine pushed the door open with a towel in her hand.

"Noooo!...don't come in…close the door…I'm naked… close the door and get out…close it…quick…" shouted Vijay.

Jasmine blushed red and putting her right palm over her mouth started to giggle. She placed the towel on the washbasin console and rushed out of the bath closing the door behind her.

That was extremely embarrassing and unacceptable for Vijay.

"Had you put the lights on, the door would have automatically got locked from inside," said Jasmine as she saw Vijay entering the hall with his head down and totally overcome with shame and humiliation.

"I'm sorry...I shouldn't have come here in the first place," Vijay mumbled without looking up at Jasmine.

"Why, what happened? What are you so much ashamed of?"

"No...nothing..."

"Look Vijay, you are married and I am married! We have seen our partner's bodies inside out. So, what is there to hide anymore? Do you have anything more special than a normal male? I confess...I don't. So, why are you so down Vijay, c'mon, be a sport and smile," said Jasmine with her arms wide open, expecting Vijay to get in there. But Vijay didn't move an inch from where he stood.

This was the first ever horrible cultural shock–a 'Clash of Culture', Vijay was experiencing.

"I have to rush home, I'm late already. We can meet some other time," Vijay said in a low voice while combing his hair.

In the meantime, with both hands clasped behind her, Jasmine quickly leaned against the main door halting Vijay's exit. Tears flowed from her blue-turned-reddish eyes over the chicks and landed on her breast. Vijay stood still in front of her like a statue, totally blank. Yet his compassionate heart saw innocence, genuineness and remorse with charm in her beautiful eyes.

Vijay put his head down and started to brisk-walk back home. He was shaken up. His body trembled as he visualized his 'nude show', the most unique scene of his life, barely ten minutes back.

All the way her words started to ring in his mind incessantly: *...we've seen our partner's bodies inside out...so, what is there to hide...what is there to hide... do you have anything more special than a normal male?... what is there to hide...anything special?...*

Perhaps she was right! She seems to have transcended the physical entity of human person and gone into spiritual. She is plain factual, down to earth, yet emancipated. Perhaps she is more moral and spiritual than I am! Thought Vijay at the end of his restlessness.

"Hi Dad, you're late today," greeted Sanjay as he saw Vijay climbing the wooden railing of his house.

"Hey Sanju, I ventured a little further in the locality and got lost among the circles, avenues and streets," Vijay excused.

"I told you in the beginning itself, either to call me or to find your way by feeding our address in Google Earth map. It would leave you at our doorsteps!" Sanjay reminded Dad.

"Yeah...I took it as a challenge, Sanju. I may not have mobile with me all the time, you see," Vijay ended the matter there itself.

Vijay threw himself on bed face up and started to look blank at the ceiling. He could not make out any damn thing off the female: Living alone without husband...feigning ownership of children that belong to her cousin...being alone in the house and inviting a stranger? Vijay was totally confused. His Indian cultural upbringing did not permit such a kind of behaviour.

Vijay thought of two alternatives. Either abort evening walks and exercise at home on the lawn or change the venue. There was no dearth of parks in surrounding area.

But...Jasmine had his mobile number. If he stopped abruptly she would definitely call him...and if that happened in Maria's presence, the cat would be out of the bag. That bag would be so much blown out of proportion that it would take a lifetime for Vijay to deflate it and prove his innocence. Vijay was surely caught in the cobweb!

Maria entered the bedroom and said, "My Viju darling, I see you very quiet these days, what's the matter with you? Are you missing Vasai or someone there?"

"Put that question to yourself, Maria! Where do you have time for me? You're so busy with changing Ajay's nappies, bathing and massaging him, making milk formulae, special cooking for lactating Nilufer, besides cooking meals for all of us. When Sanjay takes us out to Malls you are watching shelves and selecting things by yourself without even bothering to ask me if I need anything. Are you nearing your menopause dear?" Vijay said in a teasing manner.

"Shut up, you men think of that only," said Maria and got up from the bed to go to the kitchen for cleaning and cooking.

"Brother dear, tomorrow India celebrates 67th Republic Day and you said it's also some Day in Australia and you said you were planning some outing for us," said Judith over family dinner.

"Yeah Judy, it's Australia Day too. It is the official National Day of Australia celebrated same like ours on 26 January. It marks the anniversary of the 1788 arrival of the First Fleet of British Ships at Port Jackson, New South Wales, and the raising of the Flag of Great Britain at Sydney Cove by Governor Arthur Phillip," said Sanjay and continued: "I was planning to take you all to Werribee Zoo in Melbourne east."

"Oh ok, how far is it from Clayton? Will Nilu and baby go with us?" Judith asked.

"No…no…don't expose my baby to that animal zoo. Ajay baby may suffer from allergies…" Maria declared firmly.

"Ajay's Godma Rosie is visiting us tomorrow, so I'll be home anyway," Nilu intervened.

"Brother, what all animals can we get to see there?" asked Judith inquisitively.

"Well, it will take one and a half hour to reach there. There are camels, rhinos, gazelles, oryx, ostriches, giraffes, bison, deer, black bucks, meer cats, lions, monkeys, gorillas, kangaroos and various kinds of birds too," Sanjay announced in one breath.

"I'll get up early and make some Tuna sandwiches for us," Maria declared.

Judith volunteered to prepare chicken-mayo-sandwiches, because baby Olivia doesn't eat fish.

Vijay didn't have an appetite for food but pretended to munch something. He took an apple and went to the living room and sat on the sofa in front of the widescreen TV set. An important and urgent task lay ahead in abeyance, namely to text message Jasmine about tomorrow's plans, lest she called and messed up everything.

He checked WhatsApp messages and then sent one for Jasmine:

'Family outing to Werribee Zoo tomorrow. Do not call'. V

'Will miss you...come early, so v can meet'. J

'Sos...bye...GN', scribbled Vijay in hurry as he saw Judith approaching him.

Nilufer put Ajay to sleep and Judith also tried the trick with daughter Olivia.

*****

Being a national holiday, the Werribee Zoo, spread over a vast expanse of land, was still overcrowded. The parking lots were all occupied. The D'Souza clan had jolly good time at the Zoo and returned home fatigued. The Indian guests opined that the standard of zoos in Thailand, Malaysia and Singapore was much higher. They were systematically presented and compacted with more animals and birds. From one to ten, the Werribee Zoo stood at six and a half counts!

XVI

The next morning at day-break Vijay found himself mentally stressed. 'To be or not to be' at the Park in the evening, was his greatest dilemma and anxiety. As Maria prepared steamed coffee for him, Vijay checked his mobile.

'Missed you very badly yesterday...was itching to talk...but controlled ...longing for evening.'

Vijay thought he should not answer that message. But on second thoughts he warned her:

'ok, but don't ever call on this number'.

Vijay was outspoken and would not hide anything from the family but for Maria's narrow-mindedness. He would evade pointless arguments that disturbed the peace in the house. He wished evening would never fall!

Time did not stop for Vijay. He was half way through with his work-out when Jasmine entered the Park and waved at him with a restrained smile.

"Hi, how are you and how was the outing at the Zoo?" said Jasmine while making place for Vijay on the bench as he approached after the routine.

"Oh, ok…we had a jolly good time, but due to high temperature it was tiring," Vijay said.

"It's hot here too, let's go home and cool down a bit," said Jasmine and stood up.

"Jasmine, can we not talk here rather than go home?"

"That day you came and rushed out without having anything in my house. We'll have some snacks and tea or coffee, please" said Jasmine in a pleading tone.

"Come this way to the car please."

"Oh, you brought your car today, it's a big one," said Vijay in appreciation.

"Yeah, it's Honda Camry. Car is a must for easy mobility. I can drop you home, so you won't be late for your Maria," Jasmine taunted.

With the mention of Maria Vijay became apprehensive and did not answer back until they reached Jasmine's residence within a couple of minutes. The house was already cooled and very pleasant with a spray of mild freshener.

"What will you have…tea or coffee?"

"I will go for coffee."

Jasmine went to the kitchen, poured milk in two mugs and placed them in the micro. While returning she brought a plate full of Punjabi Samosas.

"C'mon have some Samosas, you'll feel you are in India,' Jasmine said proudly while holding the plate in front of Vijay.

Vijay took one Samosa from the plate and a tissue from the box Jasmine was holding in her left hand.

"Oh, they are warm and smell tempting. From where did you get them?" Vijay asked.

"There are dozens of Indian and Pakistani eateries in Clayton market area and grocery stores too. Every Indian thing is available here and the best quality."

"And I hear many Australians have taken a liking to Indian spices, especially the Indian Curry."

"Yeah, just like in the United Kingdom, here too the Indian Curry has come in vogue," added Jasmine.

"Jasmine, the other day I had seen a framed photograph on the curio cabinet of a couple holding a baby. I find it missing today."

"Oh yeah, I had removed it to wipe and forgot to place it back," said Jasmine trying to hide the fact that she didn't want Vijay to see it.

"May I see who the beauties are?"

"Hold on a second, I will get it for you," said Jasmine and rushed to her bedroom to fetch it. Coming out of the room she stretched the photo frame towards Vijay and said, "Look…these are my parents holding me when I was barely three."

"Wow, you look cute…and your mother too. She looks very Australian, doesn't she?"

"Why do you say so?"

"From her features–blue eyes and the height."

"Why, Indians don't have blue eyes and height?" said Jasmine in an effort to hide the fact that her mother was not actually an Indian.

"They do…but there is marked difference in complexion and personality."

"Yeah, my Daddy also looks cute in his Punjabi dress and Imperial moustache with curvatures at both ends. Have one more Samosa please, I'll get the coffee," Jasmine coaxed Vijay in order to change the topic.

By the time Vijay gobbled down the snack and coffee, Jasmine brought in a huge album of her wedding pictures.

"Vijay do not feel jealous of me while watching these wedding photos," Jasmine said and sat next to him on the couch.

Vijay did not comment on Jasmine's audacious statement, pretending not to have heard it.

"When did you get married?"

"Five years ago, in the Catholic Church."

In a flash second, Vijay guessed her age at thirty.

"Oh, so you got converted, Jasmine?" asked Vijay in disbelief.

"Not exactly."

"What you mean 'not exactly'?"

"You see, I grew up with both religious influences. When I was small my father occasionally took me to the Gurudwara for *Sangat* (Sikh Congregation). But most often I accompanied my Mother to the Catholic Church for religious services."

"So, you must be a very pious person?"

"Vijay, I strongly believe that all religions lead to the same One God. It doesn't make any difference if I worship Christ or Krishna. According to our holy *Granth* (The

Holy Book) Sikhs believe that there is only one God who belongs to all religions. God has no gender and therefore He is indescribable. No single religion can claim to be the only true way to Waheguru and various religions are just different ways to reach that Waheguru." Jasmine said in one go.

"So what's your Christian name?"

"Jennifer, they call me Jenny?"

"Who they?"

"Jim and his people."

"You must be going to the Church then," Vijay guessed.

"Earlier yes, but later with my flying job I could only go on occasions!" Looking at Vijay's perplexed face Jasmine said, "But why are you surprised? There are many people who do this. At the end what matters is the love between husband and wife, religion comes secondary," said Jasmine whilst trying to clear his mind.

"I find it difficult to understand how one person can live with two identities," said Vijay.

"It's easy."

"How?

"Just don't think about it!" both of them laughed heartily at Jasmine's statement.

As Jasmine opened the album, 'Wedding March' tune started to play. It was a close-up portrait of Jim and Jasmine, a beautiful couple in front of the Altar. Jasmine looked like a fairy in that white wedding gown and netted veil with the crown on her head. Jim in blue suite also looked extremely handsome with very imposing personality.

"Wow, you look the most beautiful woman in the world," said Vijay in appreciation.

She flipped pages of nuptial blessing ceremony in the Church faster and stopped at the reception function where Jasmine was dressed up in Punjabi Salwar Kameez ethnic outfit. Jasmine looked astoundingly fabulous and graceful lady. She wore a golden Phulkari –embroidered- Kurta reaching below the knees and a heavily embroidered stiff round red gown with a scarf draped over the left shoulder and under the right, and golden coloured Jutti shoes. She wore long Swarovski Dules type earrings adding sparkles to her pretty face.

Whereas Jim wore a close collar golden Sherwani in Phulkari embroidery reaching below the knees, a tight red Lehenga and Jutti shoes with extended curved tip. He also wore orange coloured heavily twisted cloth Turban giving him a look of a Maharaja.

While Vijay was engrossed in watching the pictures of beautiful guests at the wedding, Jasmine instinctively inched closer towards him. She had mentally travelled into her youthful romantic period that she was now unfolding.

Vijay felt the soft feel of her left boob at the right hand elbow. He remained still like a statue and closed his eyes to plan his next move. Before he could open them, Jasmine's lips reached near his to gauge acceptance or rejection. Vijay did not respond to her move and further kept his eyes closed.

In order to come out a winner from this disastrous attempt in trapping a lover, Jasmine suddenly got up from the couch and said: "Hey Vijay do you like Music?"

He shook his head into a 'Yes'.

"What kind"?

"Oldies…slow numbers."

Jasmine selected the numbers from her mobile and switched on the JBL Bluetooth Speaker. That was Englebert Humperdinck's last waltz. Music and dance was Vijay's passion or rather a weak point. With the strong bass and clear lyrics the air filled with serenity and romance. This trick had worked well on Vijay, Jasmine thought and instead of him asking her for a dance she approached him and pulled him up with the right arm. Instantly Vijay's right hand went around Jasmine's waist and they started to waltz.

Vijay almost went into a trance with Jasmine taking a one, a two and three steps in a perfect manner with turns, twists and pivots at the right time and place. He Karaoked the lyrics along with the singer, especially the refrain: "I had the last waltz with you / Two lonely people together / I fell in love with you / The last waltz should last forever."

Jasmine did not spare the prospects of getting as close to Vijay as possible. The Bluetooth number had ended, yet both in a tight embrace, had kept on swinging left and right. Jasmine was in the ether world, wanting to get even higher, whereas Vijay was more preoccupied with his morality as snapshots of Maria and others in the family started to appear on the screen of his mind.

Releasing her from his hands Vijay said: "Thanks Jasmine. I danced after a long break. You dance very elegantly with perfect steps, Jasmine."

"Oh, the pleasure is mine, darling, you're most welcome anytime," said Jasmine.

XVII

As planned, Jasmine dropped Vijay a block before Fulton Street at the corner of Colin Road.

While returning she cursed herself at the failed attempt of hooking this innocent looking fish. She was about to consume the pleasure of such romance, which she had missed for quite some time. She couldn't control the feminine urge for love and passion.

Biologically sexual activity is a natural urge in rational and irrational animals that works as a stimulant which causes release of Dopamine hormone in certain areas of the brain. It creates ultimate pleasurable feeling in a person. Such feeling is very addictive. It is nature's way to bring male and female together in order to procreate its progeny. Males and females instinctively choose their own preferred partners for this purpose. Apart from this, humans also use some kinds of foods, herbs and drugs to stimulate dopamine release for pleasurable activities, which can become very addictive.

Vijay entered the house only to face domestic infantry's questions and counter-questions being fired from several guns. Maria was leading the platoon. But Vijay had also prepared his counter. His newfound Indian friend Bhupinder Singh at the Princess Highway Reserve Park always served as an alibi.

"But Dad, it just takes one minute to call Mom or me to say you're visiting your friend Singh and going to be late. You simply keep us worrying about you," Sanjay said in certain stern voice.

"Am I a kid to get lost? It's almost a month and I already got the bearing of the area. Sanju give me some breathing space, ok?" Vijay said in defence.

"What breathing space? Do you get suffocated in the house here?"

"Yeah sure…everyone's busy with their chores. There is no communication, except when we eat…that too invariably about food and the dishes you see on the TV shows," retaliated Vijay and continued with a louder voice: "Outside you breathe in fresh air, converse with flowers, respond to chirping of the birds, watch children play in the Park. Ideas of a writer grow on such fertile land and not in the constricted four walls of the house with perennial naggings," the last two words being directed to taunt Maria.

With this soliloquy there was a pin-drop silence. No one said a word after that. Nilufer eyed Sanjay to get in their bedroom.

Once again that night went unbearably tough for Vijay. Jasmine's parting statement kept on ringing in Vijay's mind the whole night. "The moment I saw you in the Park I fell in love with you."

Magpie: Look out Vijay; you do not know this female well and her intentions. She is robbing you from your dearly beloved Maria for her own end. It's not too late. Stop here before you get deeper in the shit.

At this moment Vijay remembered leeches that struck on both his legs while excursing in deep jungles of Mahabaleshwar during heavy Monsoons of July. The creatures crept up inconspicuously from slippery roads covered with moss. They sucked blood and bloated. *Could Jasmine turn out to be a blood-sucker,* he wondered.

Sanjay had plans for the family next day evening. It was The Chinese New Year celebrations in Melbourne city.

*****

During the Australian Gold Rush of mid-nineteenth century (1851) large numbers of Chinese immigrants started to arrive in Australia and have never stopped till date. Living in ghettos and without diluting their own culture, the Chinese integrated themselves into the mainstream Australian polity and economy. Chinese presence and influence of their heritage in Australia has spread ubiquitously and provides a unique chapter in the history of Australia.

Traditionally the Chinese community in Australia celebrates Chinese New Year in the form of Melbourne Festival. Each New Year is dedicated in honour of an animal. Year 2017 was declared Chinese Year of the Rooster which fell on 28 January. The celebrations began from New Year Eve that is 27 January to 12 February 2017 at different landmarks of the city with variety of programmes.

The official Chinatown festival opening was on 29 January at 11 am on the corner of Russell and Little Bourke streets and followed by cultural performances into the evening. The dragon 'Dai Loong' emerged from the Chinese Museum at 11.30 pm on Sunday and paraded down Little Lonsdale Street performing a traditional dragon dance accompanied by Chinese drumming.

The Chinese Lunar New Year was celebrated at Queen Victoria Market on 28 and 29 January with traditional performances from local and international acts, including the Chinese Youth Society of Melbourne Lion Dance Team, and free cooking demonstrations.

XVIII

"C'mon…c'mon...everybody get ready? Let's get going…the Chinese won't wait for us…they start the procession sharp at five," announced Sanjay as he entered the house with his usual rush after returning from office.

With the baby seat already fixed to the hind seat, only three more persons could be accommodated in the car. So, Vijay and Nicky volunteered to travel by Metro.

It was an exciting and smooth ride from Clayton to domed Edwardian Flinders Street Railway Station, from where the Queen Victoria Market could be reached five blocks away by Tram. There were no swarms of people getting in and getting out like the local trains in Indian cities. Passengers disembarked at intended stations and others boarded the train with ease. There were ample seats and standing space available. People either read something or co-travellers dialogued but in soft voice. They do not shout while talking or sing Bhajans in the trains, like in Mumbai!

"Sanju how far are you? We've already reached and waiting near the entrance of QVM," Vijay phoned Sanjay to ensure that he and Nicky had reached the destination safely.

"I'm just parking the car, Dad…we'll be there in two minutes," said Sanjay.

In the meantime a crowd was busy watching a magic show on the road in front of the Market. People of all shapes, colours and sizes in various costumes had gathered for the Chinese festival.

The D'Souza clan reached the spot sharp at 5 pm. The drums sounded at a distance indicating that the huge parade had already started on its course from China Town to pass through the gigantic Queen Victoria Market, a historic venue situated on Queens Street in Melbourne.

The cultural kaleidoscope on this auspicious day included dragon and lion processions, cooking demonstrations and food stalls. The main attraction this year being a display of Zodiac Spectacular in the Atrium Crown Towers showcasing a fire Rooster to mark the Zodiac for 2017.

In place of regular stalls of the market, there were hundreds of make-shift food stalls put up for the public. Besides Australian lamb and pork roast, American chicken and turkey barbeque, there were Spanish, Indian, Sri Lankan, Cypriot, Mexican, Thai, Chinese, Korean, Vietnamese, et al, stalls selling their typical ethnic cuisine and national dishes.

As a band of drummers went on beating full sized drums, huge dragon and lion mascots kept up the rhythm with each stride. As the procession went further on Elizabeth Street and sound of drums diminished, the spectators returned to the food stalls to gorge on variety of food items being served to celebrate the Chinese New Year.

"Let us all be together, lest someone gets lost in the crowd. We'll go inside the market where the music is being played," said Sanjay while pointing at a group on the stage, where a lady crooner sang Country Western songs, accompanied by lead and bass guitarist and a drummer. After half an hour of listening pleasure, Pop Asia DJs took to the stage, followed by Chinese dancers and singers.

"Are you all not feeling hungry? Let's have some snacks," said Sanjay and seated his people at a vacant table and chairs. "Mom, just see what is available in these food stalls around and place an order for whatever you like," requested Sanjay.

"You know better what to order, Sanju," Maria said in a resigned manner.

"Today Mom is having a holiday from the kitchen, you relax Mama," said Judith winking at Maria.

"Let's look around Nicky. Almost all the stalls are crowded. We need to buy coupons to place an order. It will take some time for our order to get ready," said Sanjay knowing the system at these festivals.

"Ok, so you give order for barbeque while I order for some Mexican Pizzas," said Nicky and proceeded to further stalls.

Vijay, folding both his hands behind and taking slow mini-steps, was enjoying the hustle-n-bustle of the place.

"Hello brother, how are you," said a voice directed at him.

Vijay looked at the young man in his 30's with a surprise but cautioned himself when he saw him wearing a loose Pakistani style Lehenga and a Kameez.

"Yea, I'm good, how about you?" Vijay reciprocated the greeting in a gentlemanly manner.

The youth switched over to Hindi and said confidently but just to confirm, "You all must be from India!"

'Oh yeah, we are Indian from Mumbai," it was always easier to say Mumbai rather than Vasai, which was hardly 50 km away, plus many would not have heard about Vasai village.

"Where are you from?"

"I am from Afghanistan," said the youth having bushy moustache and caterpillar type thick semicircular eyebrows.

"What do you do?" asked Vijay.

"I have a stall selling handy household knick-knacks and souvenirs."

"Are you on PR or a jumper?" Vijay used a lingo usually referred to those working on cruise-liners and never returning before the liner leaves the port.

"Na...na...na...I was born in Brisbane and doing business in Melbourne. I am an Australian citizen by birth. My forefathers came to this barren land 170 years ago," said the Afghani proudly, just short of twisting his moustache like in Hindi movies.

"Oh my Gosh, then how do you speak Hindi? What's your name?" Vijay fired double barrel question.

"I'm called Javed...Javed Akhtar Khan. We have a big Muslim community of Afghans, Pakistanis and Indians living here. They converse in Pashtu, Urdu or Hindi respectively and we all understand each other very well," said the young man.

"Have you been to Afghanistan anytime?"

"No Sir..."

"Are you married? And how many children do you have?" Vijay bowled a Yorker with which Javed felt shy and sneakily started looking up on almost 40 feet tall steel ceiling structure of the Victorian styled Market.

After a pause, he slyly smiled and said, "No, sir. I'm still a bachelor. Here it is not easy to get married."

"What you mean not easy? Here we see so many girls from the subcontinent, don't you have anyone from your ethnic group?" said Vijay.

"Our girls are here but they are also not honest, we cannot rely on anyone here. These days everyone has become same. No marriages last for long. They break-up every five days. This society has gone to dogs. No morality is being practised in Australia these days. What is the use of getting married when girls don't remain in the family for lifetime?" said Javed in broken sentences on a serious note.

"What you mean rely on anyone? Don't you have proposed marriages with social bindings here, like we have back home?"

"Even if they are proposed, the outside world and its temptations are too alluring not to succumb to. It's unfortunate that present young generation does not uphold any of the age-old value system in its lifestyle. Here everyone has become individualistic and so called liberated. Nobody honours or values anyone. Their ultimate aim in life is very materialistic, to enjoy sex, drugs and live life for the present. Family life is totally collapsed in this God forbidden land," said Javed with a sympathetic face revealing total disgust.

"Are you married, Sir?"

"Yeah..."

"Is that your family (meaning wife)?"

"Yeah...and this is my darling daughter and her daughter Olivia. My son and son-in-law are fetching some snacks for us," said Vijay.

"See how beautiful your family is! How loving and caring your wife is...for you, your children and their children too." With a short pause Javed asked, "Do you live in Australia?"

"No, we are visiting our son...there he is...Sanjay and Nicky – my daughter's husband," said Vijay in case Javed did not understand 'son-in-law'.

"How beautiful family!" Javed said and continued, "There is love among all of you as a whole family. And here there is nothing of the kind. Everything's artificial and just a show-business! Everyone is selfish and wants to enjoy life."

'This guy must have had a divorce or love-break or been ditched by a fiancée or two. He must have had bitter love-separation in his prime youth and now out of disgust generalizes the situation', thought Vijay in the rear part of his brain while listening to Javed.

"Where is your shop?" asked Vijay.

"Right towards the end, but today we're closed for the Chinese New Year celebrations. You may visit my shop any day during the week," he said.

Javed is a direct descendent of 'Afghans' or also called 'Ghans' who came to Australia in 1860s as Cameleers or Caravaners. At that time the Indian Sub-Continent consisted of present-day half a dozen countries. Therefore, the Afghans who came to Australia included people from Afghanistan, Punjab, Baluchistan, Sindh, Kashmir and Rajasthan, also from countries like Egypt, Persia and Turkey.

Before the building of railways and the widespread adoption of motor vehicles, camels were primary means of bulk transport in the 'Outback Australia', where the climate was too harsh for horses and other beasts of burden.

The first Afghan cameleers arrived in Melbourne in June 1860, when three men arrived with a shipment of 24 camels for the Burke and Wills expedition. From 1860 to 1900, Afghani camel handlers played an important role in opening up Central Australia, helping in building of telegraph and railway lines.

Apart from providing vital support to exploration and settlement of the arid interior of the country these cameleers played a major role in establishing Islam and building the country's first mosque in 1861 at Marree in South Australia.

*****

Sanjay and Nicky brought loads of food-stuff, chilled water and Pepsi-Cola and lay on the table. Maria and Judith served the male members of the family and then helped themselves, as per Indian tradition. Thus the D'Souza clan celebrated the Chinese New Year of the Rooster 2017.

As the D'Souza's were feasting on the international cuisine there appeared a Punjabi family and stood near the table.

"Hi Vijay Sir, glad to see you here. Is this your family?" asked Bhupinder Singh.

"Oh yeah...this is my wife Maria, son Sanjay, his wife Nilufer with baby Ajay, my daughter Judith, her husband Nicky and their daughter Olivia," said Vijay in one go.

"Hi guys...I am Bhupinder from Haryana, I met Vijay at the Park, my wife Priti, son Amarpreet and daughter Jashleen. Hope you are having good time," said Bhupinder.

"Oh...come...come...Mr. Singh, join us for snacks," said Sanjay, though there wasn't much left.

"You all carry on, we are already done and baby is feeling sleepy, so we'll make a move," said Bhupinder and bid good-bye to the D'Souza clan.

Sanjay had instructed Vijay and Nicky just to reverse the journey in order to get back home. Besides indicators at the entrance of the Station, an announcement was being made that Springvale train was arriving on platform six.

There were not many passengers in the train at that late hour of the night.

"Nicky, watch out...Clayton comes two stations before Springvale," said Vijay apprehensive of the fact that first-time travel in a new area invariably confuses persons with regard to the bearing of directions.

Vijay had taken a window seat and kept on looking out blindly without saying a word.

"What's the matter Daddy...you look so serious?" said Nicky.

"No, nothing in particular... just watching the traffic pass-by parallel to the train track."

"See if you can spot Sanjay's car," joked Nicky.

Whereas Javed Akhtar Khan had refused to move out of Vijay's mind. Javed's woes revealed present day reality in Australia and very much in consonance with the turmoil that had exploded in Jasmine's life. Each word of his was true when applied to the present generation.

Suddenly Vijay's mind got attuned to the music of Englebertian Waltz! Those blissful moments...her sweet passionate kiss...that uncontrollable tight hug...the assurance of dying for each other...Vijay was reliving that irresistible ether-world experience once more!

As the train entered Clayton Station Nicky shook up Vijay saying, "C'mon Daddy...stop dreaming...we've reached."

Within the difference of 10 minutes the D'Souza clan got back to 504, Fulton Street at Oakleigh, Clayton.

*****

Thereafter, whenever it was feasible for Sanjay he took his visitors to show the charm of various landmarks of the world's 'Most Liveable City' – Melbourne. They included: the Eureka Tower, the City's tallest building, representing the Eureka Rebellion that ushered in Austrian democracy; the heart and soul of Melbourne life since 1878, the largest open-air market in the Southern Hemisphere – 'The Queen Victoria Market'. There Sanjay's visitors purchased gifts and souvenirs for friends and relatives back home in Vasai.

The D'Souza's also visited one of the city's top attractions – 'Sea Life Melbourne Aquarium', located on the bank of the Yarra River. They learnt more about the city from dinosaurs to early computers when they visited the 'Melbourne Museum'. They had a day-long excursion to meet 'The Twelve Apostles', a collection of limestone stacks off the shore of Port Campbell National Park, by the Great Ocean Drive. But they could see only eight of them, four having collapsed during the course of time. And finally, the cricket-loving Indians couldn't have missed the 'Melbourne Cricket Ground', the birthplace of Test Cricket'!

XIX

Vijay had got ready to step out for evening walk. While picking the mobile to shove in his pocket he noticed Jasmine's message from the corner of his eyes, but shunned any expression on the face. He knew Maria waited on him to close the main door after him.

Vijay walked faster till he reached the Colin Road corner and out of Maria's sight, in case she kept a watch on him. He slowed pace and opened the message.

"Not well…skip exercise…come home directly…miss you."

He read it again. At first he thought of pretending not to have seen the message, but on second thoughts he knew that Jasmine was smart enough to notice the two blue tick marks indicating that the message had been viewed.

Vijay got perplexed and could not decide what to do. He planned to go to the park first, do some quick work-outs and pay Jasmine a flying visit. However, when he reached the bifurcation at Ferns Street corner, instead of taking a left turn to enter the Park, his feet automatically turned to the right that led to 202, Ross Street.

Jasmine had kept the main door ajar as usual, so Vijay didn't have to ring the door bell. Vijay stood in front of the door and gently pushed it inwards. He saw Jasmine lying on the couch with her eyes closed.

Wow, isn't she gorgeous! Is it real or fantasy? What a sleeping beauty! Such an innocent face, spotless and without any stain!

Magpie: What are you doing here, in this young lady's house? Get out, you don't belong here.

Shut up, please. Leave me alone.

The carpet helped Vijay take a few tip-toed gentle steps like a thief. He stood next to the couch beside Jasmine and wondered what must have gone askew.

"Hi, when did you come?" said Jasmine in a low voice while opening her eyelids just a few millimetres.

"How did you know I was here, you were fast asleep," said Vijay to indicate that she was feigning sleep.

"I smelt you; though I am not well, I felt vibrations of your presence." Stretching her right hand Jasmine said, "Give me a hand Vijay."

"No…no…don't sit up. Relax and you take rest. I'll sit in front of you on a chair," said Vijay timidly.

"What's the matter with you Jasmine?"

While sitting up on the couch and putting both her palms over her face Jasmine rested her elbows on her laps, bent a bit and started to cry loudly, "I'm totally collapsed… my dear…I get hallucinations the whole night and cannot get a wink's sleep…I don't know what's wrong with me, darling."

She continued with the same forte, "I see him coming to attack me, to smack me, to pull me forcibly on bed and tear my night gown from top to bottom…"

Having taken a small pause to clear her nose Jasmine cried frenziedly, "I shout and scream…I fight back…but he's too bulky and strong…I get scared…he is a brute…a monster…when he clutches me in his huge arms I almost get choked…almost out of breath."

"Oh my God…! What are you talking about? Who's he?"

Vijay was flabbergasted with Jasmine's sudden outbreak. He could not decipher whether she was genuine or faking.

"That's not love…that's lust…pure carnal lust like an object…like a slave. That bastard abused me like a slave ever since our first wedding night. His house was worse than hell for me. I didn't want to live any more…it was better to die than to live a dreadful life like that. I see all those things happening in my dreams." Exasperated with her condition, with this soliloquy, Jasmine huffed heavily like a blacksmith's bellows.

"Jasmine, take it easy, I'm temporary in this place. You must be having your own people, why don't you involve some of them to solve your problem. Perhaps you may have to go to a Counsellor or the Parish Priest where you got married," said Vijay sympathetically.

"Now listen to me Vijay, all men are same. Nobody does anything for anybody without any gain. Even some of the priests are not what they are supposed to be. They will charge for the services they render, but when it comes to real question of life and death they put their hands up in surrender. They say you must suffer whatever has come your way and that's what the Holy Spirit wants you to go through. You will be rewarded in heaven at the last judgment."

"They are right in a way, for it is the Church's teaching!" said Vijay to the contrary.

"Who really knows about the Last Judgement, Vijay? Who has time to wait till then! I want justice here and now while I'm alive. I don't want empty promises after I am dead and gone!" said Jasmine with the same fury.

"If you will not mind, I'll take you to the Priest at our Parish for counselling," volunteered Vijay.

"I don't want to see any of the priests."

"Why do you talk so bitterly against those holy priests?" said Vijay with some sympathy for priests in general.

"All are not holy as you assume, Vijay. One of them molested me when I was just nine, in the AGG (Altar Girls' Guild). Haven't you read in the news about so many incidents of paedophilic priests all over the world?" said Jasmine while upping her eyebrows.

Jasmine taking a deep breath continued further, "It was a bolt from the blue when he fondled me, a terrible shock. My nerves system stopped functioning at that moment. The brain's motor system went haywire and didn't function. Nerves at the larynx got jammed and the throat got choked. No defensive cry could be produced. The sanctity of the place added to the woes."

Jasmine wiped her eyes and nose with tissues and continued: "I could not resist at that time because it was beyond my imagination and unexpected from a priest, who otherwise is supposed to be our model. Only the motor nerves of my eyes functioned incessantly and poured out some water…you may call them tears…but for the habitual abuser that amounted to plain saline water!"

"Oh my Gosh…then what really happened," asked Vijay with a serious intent.

"That excited crazy creature didn't stop at that…he started to grope downwards. I tried to shout and release myself from his clutches, but he pressed my mouth very hard. Cheeks between my teeth and his hard fingers pained me badly. Then he lifted me like a doll and placed on his laps. There was something very hard on his laps which hurt my buttocks. I did not know what it was till my adolescence. I was so close to losing my virginity, if the doorbell did not ring. Now I dread, that would have been inexplicably impossible thing in the world or a certain death for me!"

With intermittent jolty moans Jasmine continued: "He wanted to crush the bud before it could bloom into a flower. What right did he have to touch me? Just because he was a Priest with authority to do anything he wished? Just because no one would know whatever happened within the four walls of his room? Where were his conscience, Christian values and morality he preached from the pulpit?"

Vijay was completely stupefied…bowled out and tried to pacify her: "Why didn't you complain to his Superior?"

"What Superior? I wouldn't dare complain even to my own parents. Even if I took a chance, they would not believe me. They would conclude I have done something wrong somewhere and trying to push it on the Priest. So much blind faith these people have in the priests. But, tell you, such nasty paedophilic priests would have a slightest chance of entering heaven, if at all there exists one!"

"Jasmine, cool down a bit...look...there may be just two percent of the fold who falter, but there are ninety eight per cent who are doing marvellous work both spiritual and humanitarian. Why do you generalize because of a few exceptions? What nationality was the priest, Jasmine?" asked Vijay inquisitively.

"Sorry Vijay. I can't reveal his identity. We have had, Aussies, Americans, British, Indians, Pakistanis and even Lebanese, coming in and going out of our Parish. Nationality and colour does not matter. It's the human integrity and faithfulness to one's vocation. If you can't follow the edicts of an institution you are in, whether or not they are natural, unnatural or supernatural, and you insist on clinging to the profession, you become a hypocrite. You have to just get out from there before you blemish the good name of the Holy Priesthood."

Jasmine continued in the same tone, "No one should spoil innocent children under the garb of religiosity. In other words it amounts to spiritual terrorism! That also ruins the immense sacrifices of the majority who adhere to their vocation with all sincerity. Jesus has prescribed very stern retribution for such acts: 'It would be better for them to be thrown into the sea with a millstone tied around their neck than to cause one of these little ones to fall into sin.' "

"Jasmine, I can't take any more of this stuff. I am utterly bewildered right now and prefer some solitude, some space to digest all that you have said," said Vijay with modesty.

"Please...please Vijay, sit next to me and hold me. I'm shivering...give me some moral support in my trepidation," said Jasmine with joined hands.

Seeing Jasmine's exasperated condition, as a human being Vijay had no choice but to do what Jasmine wanted him to. He sat at her left and tried to console her by rubbing his right palm on her right shoulder. She rested her head on his chest. His conscience woke up. Photographic shots of Maria, Sanjay, Nilufer and Judith started to flash every second on the screen of his mind.

"Listen Jasmine, you lie down on the couch and I will make you a nice cup of hot black coffee...you'll feel better I guarantee," said Vijay in order to come out of her enticement.

"I don't want anything anymore...in life! You're God-sent for my rescue!" she said with confidence.

"But do you believe in God?"

"When needs arise people always think of God. In fact that is how they created him in the first place...to serve their purpose and justify their actions, whether good or bad. Why these things had to happen particularly to me?" said Jasmine desperately.

"What things?"

"This idiot, my husband, the sex-maniac! With that childhood experience of the priest, sex had become quite nauseating for me. I pleaded Jim time and again not to treat me like an object, but to love me like a person. But no, it didn't get into his big head what is love and how to care for his wife," she said bitterly.

"Is he aware of your childhood experience?"

"Yeah...I told him umpteen times without identifying the priest. In his fury Jim even threatened to kill the priest but he was transferred to some other place after his Bishop received complaints about his paedophilic activities."

Jasmine went on narrating the story but Vijay just nodded his head occasionally. Mentally he was not present there. His mind had travelled to the sensual encounters Jasmine had tried with him and how he had won over her allures. Or else today she would have weighed him in the same scale.

With today's episode Jasmine's murky image started to get clearer for Vijay. Perhaps her present conduct could be the result of what came upon her, he thought. Why should one blame her outright for force-de-majeure situations which were not her conscious choice?

"How many sugar?" Vijay yelled from the kitchen.

"None...just black," said Jasmine softly.

"Take a deep breath before you take each sip, Jasmine. That will work on you for tranquillity."

After she finished the coffee, Jasmine did feel better. She felt invigorated.

"You were talking about some things, Jasmine. What things bother you? You must not keep anything in mind that bothers you. Just empty it out and feel relaxed. Don't you have any confidant whom you can trust?" said Vijay on Counsellor's note.

"Both my confidants are away, Vijay."

"Who both?"

"My Mother and my Husband."

"But you said your mother had died some time back? And your husband travels to Canada?" asked Vijay with folds on his forehead.

Mr. Bhupinder Singh had been a convenient alibi at any time Vijay needed him to be. Not strictly in legal terms but from the point of view of human behavioural patterns in given family situations, Mr. Singh served an easy safety valve for Vijay.

Everything was normal when Vijay arrived home late previous night from Jasmine's residence. He had informed home in advance that he was going to help Bhupinder pack his family's bags, who were travelling home to Haryana the next day. Bhupinder could not travel with his family because he was requested by Nestle Australia to extend his stay till his replacement arrived from Singapore.

In fact Vijay remembered Bhupinder's statement when they met the first time at the Princess Highway Reserve Park saying, "There was no need of friends for I have plenty of relatives living in Australia from more than seven to eight generations before."

"But relatives and friends are on two different levels. Man or a woman always needs a friend, even if he or she is married," Vijay had said.

The next morning Vijay was up at 5 am and paraded to Bhupinder's residence to accompany the Singh's to Melbourne Airport.

After emotional goodbyes, hugs-n-kisses to his wife and children at the airport, Bhupinder Singh saw his family out of sight into the exit lounge.

"Sorry, I couldn't make it to the Park for the past couple of weeks because we were on a shopping spree," said Bhupinder in apologetic voice, as he drove homewards sluggishly through the morning traffic rush. "Do you meet that dame Jasmine in the Park?" Bhupinder asked.

"Well, I did see her there sometimes." half-confessed Vijay. "Why, what happened, why do you ask?"

"Just a warning...be careful with her. I think she's loose. She tries to come close without much previous acquaintance. She invited us to her house and we did visit her couple of times. But my wife Preeti smelt something fishy and advised me to keep distance from the female."

"Did she visit your place anytime?"

"Oh yes...we invited her for Amarpreet's birthday party last month. Well, at that time she behaved in such familiarity with people she never met before and instantly became the centre of attraction." said Bhupinder.

"So what, perhaps she has adopted Australian mannerism. We cannot judge people from their external conduct," said Vijay with a firm voice.

"I'm saying so because there is something to it, my dear Vijay Sir," said Bhupinder on an assured note.

"Oh, you have investigated her then?"

"Of course...we have so many people here. And as far as our community is concerned every secret is a public secret."

"I heard she is from Bhavani in Punjab, is she?" asked Vijay.

"Yes and no; her father, Himmat Singh, hailed from Bhavani who married a lady Akaldeep by name from the same village. He brought her here but within few months she deserted him and went back to India. Jasmine's father drove a Taxi, plying almost 18 hours a day. He was six footer, very handsome and talkative."

"Oh, very interesting indeed! Go ahead...then what happened?" Vijay coaxed him to come out with more info.

"Then...I think he found someone from here...I don't remember well, you see. These are the things we gossip while partying and once you are tipsy you tend to forget them the next morning."

"Yeah, quite true...it happens with me too," Vijay seconded him.

"Wait...hold on a second, I recollect something hazily" with a small pause Bhupinder continued, "Yes...I got it..."

"Taking rounds in the neighbourhood looking for passengers, one early morning Himmat Singh saw a pretty young lady standing alone at a corner. He slowed down the taxi and lowered the left side window glass..."

The young lady got an indication from the taxi driver and said, "No, no...thanks, I'm waiting for my pick-up."

"Himmat took rounds in couple of blocks further but did not get any passenger. But this lady kept hovering in his mind. From her dress he knew she was a Qantas

Airhostess. She looked astoundingly pretty to miss and talk to. So, he took a chance to see if she was still standing at the corner. There were no mobile phones then."

"Himmat Singh had basic education but was pushy with his unrefined English. He slowed down his vehicle near her and dared to ask, "Good Morning Ma'am...may I drop you to the airport? I am going there for a pick-up any way."

"She looked at her watch...looked around once again if the airline Coaster was in sight and then nodded to the driver indicating yes. Himmat immediately sprang from his seat, went from the rear and opened the door for the lady."

"Then what happened?" interrupted Vijay with curiosity.

While changing the lane for a right turn, Bhupinder halted Vijay with gesticulation with his left hand and after bifurcating from the Interstate Highway, he said, "Just listen to me, Sir Vijay."

"If he did not break protocols why would they call him *'Himmat'* meaning 'courage'? He sort of interviewed her with questions such as, "what is your name?", "where do you live?", "how many years' service with Qantas?", "how many siblings?", "do you live with your parents or alone?" The lady did not have choice but to oblige him with answers while in the middle of the traffic. At the airport, looking at the meter she stretched out a 100 Dollar bill towards him. But he said, "Na...doesn't matter Lady Jessica. I was going to come here anyway; and now that we happened to be neighbours, I could pick you up everyday this time."

She gave a sweet smile and said, “No, thanks a lot, we get our pick-up regularly; besides our duty varies from time to time. Bye, have a good day,” and she slammed the door. This to Himmat was a ‘sweet hurt’!

“That was the happiest day in Himmat Singh’s life after his wife Akaldeep had left him two years ago. He couldn’t have a better day than celebrating it with a couple of beers in a pub.”

“Then what happened…?” asked Vijay to satiate his curiosity.

“Then fate took its own course. Himmat had the courage to dream of this Australian beauty, day and night. He had a strong determination to trail her.”

“One day Himmat’s telephone rang in the middle of the night. “My father is dying, please come here with your car immediately,” cried Jessica over the landline phone. Himmat rushed to the next block with his Taxi car, put Jessica’s father Pete in the hind seat and took him directly to the Emergency Ward of the Monash Hospital, located close by.”

“After half an hour, the Doctor came out of the ER with morose face and declared, “Mr. Pete Smith is no more!” Hearing that, Jessica started to howl and cry very profusely. As Himmat Sing tried to calm her down and console her, she clung to him closest, perhaps not conscious of the fact that he was totally a stranger. When the nurses brought the stretcher out of ER, they were rather surprised to see this Australian beauty in the embrace of an Indian, clad shabbily in Kameez top and a loose Lehenga!”

“Jessica’s mother Sarah was home alone having fever. The mortal remains of Mr. Smith were taken directly to the Cemetery. Jessica neither had siblings, nor any relatives available to attend to the funeral. The Undertaker had only ailing Sarah, Jessica and Himmat as attendants."

"After about six months, Sarah joined her husband in heaven."

"So, Jessica was left alone to fend for herself," said Vijay with a concern.

"By then well acquainted Jessica moved in with Himmat Singh. That was about thirty years ago. 'Live-in' lifestyle wasn't prevalent even in the Western world then, and much less in these down-under countries, what they call Oceania these days. But both were dare-devils! " exclaimed Bhupinder.

"When they came to clubs, social functions or even to Church occasionally, heads turned ninety degrees left and right to confirm whether what they saw was real or a fantasy! Because Jessica dressed up for the ramp and Himmat preferred the loose Punjabi Kameez and Lehenga."

"Himmat Singh would reach and bring Jessica to and from the airport at any given time of the day or night. In social life they were an inseparable pair. Perhaps they lived a better married life than if they were officially married in a Church or a Gurudwara!"

"Within a year they got a gift of their unwedded love. After that Jessica never flew. She preferred to take up a ground job at a loss of handsome flying perks. The threesome family became pride of the neighbourhood. With her unique crossed-racial features, Jasmine as a child became darling of the Ross Street dwellers."

"Himmat was a meat-eater. Barbequed lamb chops, pork chops and T-bone steaks with beer were his favourites. He didn't really care for his physical fitness. He lived for the day."

"Just about a year ago Himmat had a massive heart attack and left Jessica and Jasmine alone. Jessica could not bear the shock and took ill with Parkinson's. She has been kept at some Home for the aged."

Bhupinder braked the car in the parking lot at a Mall where multinational food courts served ethnic cuisines.

Vijay came to his senses with the jerk and asked Bhupinder, "Where have we come?"

"I've informed my office that I would be late today. Let's have some breakfast," Bhupinder requested Vijay.

"Tell me, do you want to have a continental breakfast with sausages, salami, ham and half-fried eggs or Mexican Tacos with Chorizo or Chinese dumplings with You Tiao or Indian Idli-Wada and Masala Dosa?"

With that quick litany of food items from Bhupinder, Vijay got confused and didn't know what exactly to go for.

Magpie: *This Indian has adapted to the Australian way of life pretty well and quickly!*

Bhupinder whispered something which only the waiter could understand.

After a while, the waiter brought a plate of Wada Sambar and a plate of Punjabi Samosa. Without hesitation Bhupinder, like a villager in Punjab, pinched a Samosa from one plate between his thumb and index finger and placed it in the other plate and picked a Medu Wada from that plate and placed it in the first one. So, both had equal quality and quantity. Then he said, "Vijay Sir, you can have the Chutney and I will have the Sambar, 'cause it'll be too pungent hot for you."

While both waited for coffee to arrive Bhupinder said, "Sir, you are not yourself today. Is anything bothering you?"

"No, no…nothing's wrong; I was only thinking of that poor Jasmine. All alone, how she must be coping with things by herself without any help from anyone?"

"Children in Australia, like in Europe and Americas, are taught from their childhood to be independent. That is a huge drawback for our Indian culture. We care for sons and daughters till they get married and have children. In most cases we even worry about our grandchildren till they get married!"

Vijay just kept on stirring his coffee without saying a word. Jasmine refused to leave him alone in peace.

Bhupinder disrupted his deep thinking and said, "Don't worry about that girl, Sir. Like her mother she has seen life and knows how to face it."

"But how about her husband Jim, she talks about? Do you know anything about him? asked Vijay.

"No, not really; we have never seen him but whenever we asked about him Jasmine always gave excuses saying he was out on a study tour."

"Where? To Canada?" asked Vijay.

"The latest we heard was that he belonged to a funky club, always on drugs with homosexuals and cult rituals. From another source he was reported to have been admitted for Palliative care in the National Centre for Cancer Patients," said Bhupinder.

After breakfast on their way home Vijay asked, "How do you know all these details about her and the family?"

"It was in the Princess Highway Reserve Park, while my family waited for me in the evenings. The ladies must have exchanged their personal experiences," said Bhupinder.

"Why do you use past tense? Aren't they still friends?" Vijay inquired.

"There was a clash of cultures; Jasmine's liberal ways did not match with Preeti's conservative ones."

Magpie: You must resolve not to rash judge anyone by their external behaviour.

As Bhupinder closed on to 504, Fulton Street, Vijay said, "C'mon, say hello to Maria and have some tea or coffee."

"Not at all, thanks. We just had some…plus I need to rush to the office," said Bhupinder and zoomed away.

XXI

"Daddy quiet please, don't make that usual hullabaloo," said Nilufer as she placed her right index finger on her lips, of course with a sweet smile towards her father-in-law.

"Oh...baby's asleep? I'm sorry."

"Not Ajay Daddy, it's your baby...Mummy's got a severe headache," said Nilufer directing him with her eyes towards the bedroom.

"Hi sweetheart, what happened? Fever?" said Vijay while touching Maria's forehead.

There was no answer from her. But Nilufer whispered from the door, "I've given her two Panadols, Daddy. Let her rest for some time."

Vijay just shook his head in the affirmative and came out of the room.

"Where have the Fernandes gone today? Isn't their shopping over yet?" inquired Vijay.

"Can't imagine how the month passed so fast," Nilufer said to support Daddy.

Once Vijay got some solitude, his mind started to ruminate over the episodes he heard from Bhupinder, just like coconut, garlic, ginger, chillies and coriander that were ground together to make Chutney, Bhupinder had offered him an hour ago for South Indian breakfast. Vijay was restive over what he had heard from Bhupinder Singh, yet indifferent! Rather he genuinely wished to help Jasmine through the trauma.

Magpie: There are hundreds and thousands of such females in similar situations here in Australia. Depression is catching up with heart-attack on the chart. It has become a part of life, easily accepted and faced. Maintain your balance; else it will cost peace in your family.

Vijay and Maria could be Australia's guests only for the next forty-five days; that many had quickly passed. By now they had visited most of the landmarks in Melbourne. But places of interest such as the famous Opera House, the Gold Coast area, Capital Canberra were yet to be explored.

Vijay's initial apprehensions about Jasmine were increasingly unfolding correct. 'Being born and brought up in Bombay how can one not know that the place was also called Mumbai? Then, yarns about her husband Jim being sent on a study tour to Canada by his Company, whereas he was very much here in some Reform Home! The initial claim she faked that Sarika and Surjit were her own children?'

A soft jingle rang on Vijay's mobile with a message:

"Going to see Mom this evening, come prepared."

Magpie: See, first she used to request you; now she orders. Who can order whom? One who owns the person! Now she presumably owns you. It's never too late, though.

No, no birdie, don't taunt me like this. Leave me alone, I'm being myself. I am a man of action and not just philosophising. I must plan my alibi for the evening; any ideas?

"What time?" Vijay pressed the 'Go'.

"As usual, five..." came the answer before Vijay could even take a wink.

Vijay pressed the alphabet "k" not knowing what it meant.

"Ah…Bhupinder Singh, the saviour! Thank Goodness the blessed Company extended Bhupinder's stay," Vijay said to himself.

Magpie: Now that his family has gone to India, what more work will Bhupinder want you to help him in? In fact it would now be his turn to help you somehow.

"Ok...Bhupinder's Aunt is serious and I am going to visit her...enough!" Vijay thought.

After those tablets in the morning and some hot soup, Maria felt better and was on her feet once again.

"Wow…you're dressed for a party! No exercise today?" said Maria teasingly.

"Not even a day has passed that his family left for India and this fellow, Bhupinder, has started to feel lonely. He wants me to accompany him to see his ailing Aunt." Vijay fired an alibi.

"Is she having a day-care Nurse or is she in some Home, Dad?" inquired Nilufer just out of curiosity.

That was a dilemmatic question to Vijay, just like bull's second horn, so he said, "As a matter of fact I don't have any details of his Aunt but once I get to visit her, I will tell you all about her."

Maria could sense a little nervousness in Vijay's voice. She pierced her eyes into Vijay's head and screened broken lines on the graph. But she didn't say a word and gave the benefit of the doubt to her beloved husband.

Jasmine waited for Vijay near the Park's entrance. She saw him from the side mirror brisk-walking and approaching the car. Her hand went into the purse to remove lipstick which she quickly applied on her lips; put the sun flap down and looking into its small mirror pressed the lips together.

"Hi dear, how are you today?" scurried Jasmine.

"Good… and you?" said Vijay as a routine.

"I am excited to see Mom today, it's been two weeks."

Today I will show Mom the person I fell in love at first sight at the Park. I hope she understands my taking Vijay to see her. Whether it was her approval or my bad luck, Jim the swine has ruined my life for sure. Let's not play the same old record. Jasmine thought swiftly before starting a conversation.

"How far is this place we are going to?" Vijay.

"MannaCare is located off Manningham Road, near Melaleuca Avenue at Doncaster, just about half an hour's drive," Jasmine said while taking left to cross under Princess Highway flyover. "It's a fantastic place, well maintained – clean and neat, for aging people to live in. They serve nutritious meals to inmates, have highly experienced and dedicated nursing staff."

"Your government has plenty of facilities for old people, for young children, for new-borns, for new mothers and mothers to be. Great! We in India are lacking all these benefits, because of rampant corruption by our politicians," said Vijay first with an appreciative followed by frustrated pitch.

"Yes, we pay heavy taxes and people pay government dues promptly," said Jasmine.

"Yeah, you're right…in India only one-and-half to two percent of the population pay taxes honestly and regularly." Vijay said regretfully.

'If all eligible persons paid their taxes honestly, India would become financially very strong country.' This is what I heard in a debate on 7 to 9 Breakfast TV show." Jasmine added.

By this time Jasmine had crossed Monash Freeway and proceeded towards Burwood.

"Your local City Council Office must be giving financial support for this facility, isn't it, Jasmine?" said Vijay expecting at least a nod from Jasmine but she came out vehemently, saying, "No, no…this is a not-for-profit organisation generously supported by the community and a Board of Donors.

Crossing the Eastern Freeway intersection they approached Doncaster City Council Area.

At MannaCare Jasmine pressed the door-bell and before anyone said anything Jasmine just said, "173", and 'click'… the door latch opened. She went to a corner and bent over a small stool to register the visit.

As Jasmine led Vijay to her Mom's room that crossed sitting room where several senior persons sat and viewed

TV, he found some conversed with one another without being able to hear or understand anything, some laughed heartily without humour and others just sat and dozed.

"Knock knock…anyone home," said Jasmine jokingly and opened the door. She rushed to the Easy-chair, bent herself and hugged Jessica. Vijay just stood in the door and watched this very emotional mother-daughter reunion.

As Jasmine straightened herself up Vijay saw this wrinkled yet beautiful face with blue sparkling eyes. Jessica softly smiled at him and extended her shaky hand to greet him. Vijay was just stunned to see her graceful gesture and imagined how gorgeous and elegant this female might have been in her prime youth!

Magpie: This is the tragedy of human life. Lastly all human glory becomes futile. The youthful beauty is replaced by wrinkles, the self-esteem with timidity and the arrogance with defeat. At the end people hasten to be one with the unknown, in the oblivion. People go by external physical beauty but what you are experiencing is real splendour of character.

"Mom, this is Vijay, my colleague at work." Jasmine said.

"No, no…that's not true, I'm a visitor here," Vijay wanted to interrupt Jasmine, but thought Jessica would not care about who he really was.

"Where…is he…from…Jenny?" struggled Jessica.

"Bombay, India." Jasmine said loudly. Hearing that, Jessica's face lifted up a bit. Perhaps she remembered her beloved Himmat.

But Vijay looked on the floor and tried to remember the first time Jasmine had told him that she also had a

Christian name. Her mother Jessica addressed her Jenny while father Himmat lovingly named her Jasmine. Similarly she had both Australian as well as Indian influence and upbringing in the house. Her husband Jim being in a reform home, by her thirties Jenny felt liberated from her marriage liabilities and in the second phase she desperately tried to lure an Indian mate, so to say.

MannaCare was an extremely well maintained Home, housing old men and women. At the end, human person's condition becomes very fragile, helpless and pathetic.

Trying to hold Jessica's both hands and cheering her to stand up, Jasmine said, "C'mon Mom, let's take a few steps." Looking at Vijay Jasmine said, "She's got a mild attack of Parkinson's...there are tremors in her hands... due to stiffness her movements have become slow... sometimes she seems to lose her balance."

Jessica stood almost 6 feet tall. Jasmine brought her out in the garden. Jessica felt elevated and looked refreshed. Upon their return to the self-contained room, the nurse had brought in a small cup of pudding. It was a practice of the house that close relatives of the inmates should feed them with tender loving care. The famous TLC!

"Aha...look what's here Mom! Your favourite Strawberry Pudding." Said Jasmine cheerfully and started to feed her with the spoon.

What a lovely scene this is, pure filial love! I'm edified that they still have it in here. Perhaps because of Himmat's Indian genes! Vijay thought.

XXII

"Yeah Nilufer…what's up?" Vijay answered the phone as Jasmine and he walked towards the car in the parking lot.

"Daddy, nothing's up but mom is down. She has fever again. Come home soon wherever you are," said Nilufer.

"Ok, I'll be there within an hour or so."

Jasmine opened the car door for Vijay as he was on the phone and she quickly went to the driver's side. Before he got in the car, he spotted an Indian lady being driven by an Aussie. As she came out of the car she kept staring at Vijay. But seeing Vijay's cold response, she hesitated a little and walked away to the building. Vijay too felt having seen the lady somewhere, but with Nilufer's SOS call he did not bother about her.

"Who is it dear? What's the matter? Was that call from home?" Jasmine asked as she drove the car out.

"Yeah…Maria is down again, high temperature it seems."

"Oh no, you better get her checked thoroughly in the hospital. Don't keep her just on Panadols." Advised Jasmine with a concern and said, "Shall I go with you to see her?"

"No…no...They will misunderstand us. Indians are not broad-minded like people here. They immediately come to conclusions." Vijay tried to explain the very awful Indian social attitude.

"Let them think whatever…I don't care."

"But I do care. If you do that, we will never be able to meet again," assured Vijay with confidence. With this deterrence from Vijay, Jasmine kept on driving for some time without saying anything.

To break the loud silence, Vijay said, "So, how did your mother take me accompanying you to the Home?"

"I'll tell over a cup of coffee. Do you care for one?" asked Jasmine and turned to 'Bakery & Café' on a service road.

Jasmine signalled Vijay to sit at a corner table while she went to get them coffee from the counter.

"How many cubes sugar?" she asked.

"Just half," Vijay responded quickly before she could empty the full sachet.

"Do you have Diabetes Mellitus, Vijay?

"Sort of…" said Vijay distractedly.

"What do you mean sort of? Either you have it or you don't."

"Perhaps I'm pre-diabetic."

"However, we must check your sugar," said Jasmine with authority and continued with the sugar, "I'll take one and your half. I want to drink your sweetness!" Jasmine said as she smiled with half twisted lower lip pinched between her teeth.

Coming back to Vijay's earlier question Jasmine said: "Oh, excellent, Mom liked you very much. Not with words but by her very expressions. I can assure she was very happy to meet you."

"Hope she doesn't get ideas," said Vijay with sarcasm.

"What ideas dear?"

"I hope she hasn't mistaken me for Jim, your Husband?" said Vijay with doubtful facial expression.

With that remark Jasmine abruptly stopped stirring her coffee, made big eyes at him and said, "Vijay she isn't down with Alzheimer's but Parkinson's. She recognises and remembers people alright!" The next moment blinking her eyes smaller Jasmine said, "But I think she must have guessed that I love you."

"That's very common word. Why do you love me?" Vijay asked.

"I already told you that I fell in love with you the first day I saw you in the Princess Highway Reserve Park," said Jasmine and slapped her palm on his shoulder in an affectionate manner.

"But why so?" Vijay persisted.

"I like you: firstly because I like the way you are, the way you look, the way you behave, the way you think, the way you talk, and secondly of course the way you love me." said Jasmine in a mischievously loving manner.

"You're pretty presumptuous! How do you know I love you? Perhaps I could be pretending to love you or like you, I may be studying you perhaps for my selfish motives." Vijay said sternly.

"Such as..." Jasmine.

"Such as you are young and smart, a good company, you are helpful, you are sweet, you are understanding and adjustable, you are compassionate and much more than anything else you are humane. Your touch, your smell, your being next to me gives me a solid reason to be, to exist...for someone like you," said Vijay in equally loving manner.

Magpie: Hey buddy; you're going overboard, even if you are feigning it. Remember, you showered the same amorous verbose flowers over Maria to win her heart before marriage? Now she is your wife for 25 years! Check your integrity and propriety.

"Gosh! You sound very pious and poetic! Now I know why I hated my husband. At first I loved him; I gave my whole self to him. But within days that so called love diminished and vanished. May be because of his certain ways that did not click with mine, and my understanding of life, the way things had to be done," Jasmine said.

"Might be that he too did not like the way you behaved and that is the reason he behaved that way with you in return. So, whether it is love or hatred, it is always reciprocal, never one-sided," said Vijay.

At this statement Jasmine made big eyes at Vijay, indicating that he was taking her husband's side.

"Why are you staring at me with big eyes? I think today I must make some things clear Jasmine."

"C'mon darling…come out…tell me, what is it?"

"I can't accept this very word 'darling'. Am I your husband or a lover for you to call me darling?" Vijay asked a genuine question that disturbed him for long.

"Ok Vijay, in our culture dear and darling are words randomly used to address persons who are quite friendly or familiar to each other. It has no other connotation," Jasmine explained.

"Yeah, for us Indians it has. For many it has romantic and sensual connotations," clarified Vijay and continued, "But an affectionate relationship into which the sexual element does not exist, is called Platonic love, especially in situations where one might easily assume otherwise." Vijay said.

"Ok then…you may call our friendship as 'Platonic Relationship' because ours is a deep yet non-sexual friendship between two heterosexual people–of opposite sex, such as you and me, done? You understand me well and I know your heart, we tune in perfectly well, don't we darl.., oh…Vijay?" Jasmine juggled words and phrases in a smart way and smiled at Vijay, as she turned the car right to come out of the Princes Highway Reserve Park to arrive at North Road.

"Jasmine, you may drop me at a block before Fulton Street at the corner of Colin Road, just like last time." Vijay said with some nervousness.

"C'mon Vijay…why are you so worried?" Jasmine tried to liven-up Vijay.

Vijay muttered, "The alibi…! It has back-fired. I'll be screwed now!"

“What did you say?...screw?” Jasmine got tickled with the word coming out of Vijay.

“No, no…I am scrupulous, I meant.”

XXIII

As Vijay entered the house he smelt the atmosphere very serene like never before.

"Where is my darling Maria? What happened to her?" Vijay touched Maria's forehead and felt it warm. "Oh, you're burning with fever my darling."

Instead of being heartbroken, Vijay put all to work as if one's wife having high temperature was a matter of routine. "Sanju, just bring the AC at a lower temperature. Nilufer, please dip Mom's washed handkerchief in salted ice-cold water and put it on her forehead. You must change it after every 10 minutes, please. Judy darling, please bring an ice-pack from the fridge and apply it all over mom's body."

Everyone did their assigned jobs and gathered for family dinner without the Lady of the house. However, she was served plain hot soup at her bedside. Vijay finished his bite quickly and came to check on Maria's fever. The temperature had gone down considerably to near normal.

Maria kept on getting these bouts of sudden high fever followed by above home treatment. One day, Judith pulled Sanjay to a side and said, “Sanjay bro, I’m worried about Mom. She needs a thorough medical check-up. There must be something deeper than what is seen on the surface with Mom.”

“And so with Dad,” added Sanjay sarcastically.

Whereas, Vijay remained faithful to his evening walks.

Sanjay and Judith had some discussion and planned to talk to their father privately.

It was a Sunday; Nicky had gone to fetch a few last minute things as they were supposed to fly to India two days thence.

“Dad, Judith and I are going to Church for Mass. Plus Judith wants to say ‘adieus’ to that Priest from Pakistan. Would you like to go with us?” proposed Sanjay with a religious tone.

“I want to do little shopping after that, brother dear,” said Judith to lure Dad.

“Ok then, I’m game,” said Vijay willingly.

After the Holy Mass got over, Sanjay and Judith took Vijay to the adjacent garden within the Church compound.

After a little hesitation on how to put it, Judith said, “Dad, it happens to many men between 40 to 55 years of age.”

“But the age differs among women,” said Sanjay looking at Judith for her concurrence.

“What are you talking about? What 40 and 55 years?”

Looking at Vijay Judith said, “Dad you should know what is midlife crisis, don’t you.”

"I certainly know what midlife crisis is, Judy! It's a critical phase when men or women reach halfway through life and face emotional upheavals. But why do you relate it to me? Do you think I'm acting weird?" Vijay said with curls on his forehead.

"Dad, are you playing innocent like a cat who drinks milk with closed eyes and thinks no one is watching it?" said Sanjay with certain confidence.

"When one does not do anything wrong, there is no need to hide it?" Judith said immediately before Sanjay could finish his sentence.

"But why are you both firing questions at me left and right? What have I hidden from anyone?" said Vijay desperately.

"What have you hidden?? Show it to Dad Sanjay..." Judith nodded her head in affirmation.

Sanjay manipulated his mobile, brought a picture on the screen and said, "Look at this registration, whose names are written on the Register of MannaCare, at Doncaster last week?

"Who's this Jenny you went with at the home for the aged last week?" asked Judith in a serious tone.

"Which Jenny ...from where?

"That name 'Vijay' is you Daddy and you went there last week with a female, did you not?" Sanjay fired the question sternly.

"I did go there but not with Jenny."

"Whoever she was but wasn't she a female?"

"Yeah...yeah...Jasmine...she is also called Jennifer by her people. So, what happened?" asked Vijay as a matter of fact.

"Nothing…! But it may happen now! Can you tell us where most of your evening walks are spent?" asked Judith.

At this point Vijay found himself being cornered from all sides and there was no easy escape. So, he decided to come out clear and loud since his conscience was clear.

"Look here fellas…don't make a mountain out of a mole. There is nothing to worry about. This lady Jasmine is in deep shit with her husband and I'm trying to help her out from her marital problems," said Vijay in a pathetic voice.

"But there was no need to tell us lies Dad…you're killing our faith in you, our confidence in you. Don't you understand, we love and respect you? Then why are you doing all such things?" Sanjay said.

"You want to know the truth? Then listen: …you were small that time…as a member of the Parish Council, I used to accompany our Parish-Priest in solving marital cases in our parish and elsewhere. You see, generally people forget that in a marital relationship man and woman have to dissolve and surrender their ego without having any competition with each other. If they don't dissolve the ego, expectations from each other increase day after day and reach such heights that fault-finding begins at every action of the partner. Then they lose the real meaning and understanding of marital relationship?"

Clearing his throat Vijay further continued, "We succeeded in settling at least eight out of ten cases of marital discord. When I used to come home late Mom used to get upset for no reason. Gradually she became suspicious and eventually stopped me from doing this very important social work of family reconciliation. She victimised me vis-à-vis doing significant community job of restoring broken families," trembled Vijay's voice from his larynx.

Both Sanjay and Judith listened to their father's soliloquy, astounded with their mouths half open in awe.

"Then what happened?" asked Judith.

"I had made a name for myself in Society. They respected my judicious way of handling things without hurting either of the party. But then I became a victim of suspicion from my own spouse. I had to give up my mission and membership of the Parish Council. I became a subordinate under your Mom's commands."

"It must have been a sudden brake on your social activities, Dad," said Sanjay.

"Certainly, all of a sudden I became a nerd and withdrawn. Many persons approached me to continue this all time important ministry. Settlement between husband and wife is very important factor for the good health of our society and of any nation. Husband-wife separation and divorce are the biggest curse on our society today. And Counselling works as a great panacea against this social evil. But I thought it was prudent to save my own marriage first, before others."

Sanjay and Judith looked at each other and then at their father with a sorry face.

Vijay continued further: "In order to camouflage this social virus they have come out with live-in system, the so-called 'Cohabitation'! My worry is that in near future this phenomenon is going to obliterate the institution of Marriage and family life absolutely from the face of the earth."

"Sorry Dad, we did not know all this history," said Judith on an apologetic note.

"Tell me, how did you come to know about my visit to the MannaCare Home?" Vijay asked.

Sanjay hesitantly said, "I received a call from that Adrian D'Mello who is involved with Scarlet, Naronha's daughter-in-law. Mom refers to her as having a loose character and detests her."

"Oh, that was the lady who was staring at me in the parking lot!" said Vijay in confirmation.

"Dad, listen what happened after that. Scarlet and Adrian work together in the same office. Though married to Sabby Naronha, she was having a fling with Adrian. Like familiarity breeds contempt, Scarlet started to ignore Adrian and developed friendship with an Aussie. Adrian wanted to prove Sabby, her husband, about her flirting and started to trail her."

Interrupting Sanjay Vijay asked, "So, how do I come into the picture?"

"Precisely you do. Adrian leaked this info to Sabby. Sabby and Scarlet had a big brawl in the house and at that time she referred to you saying, "How come that Sanjay's father is moving around with some Australian lady?" explained Sanjay.

Judith added, "Scarlet had gone to visit that Australian man's ailing mother at MannaCare. After they signed the register, Adrian sneaked in saying he was with that couple and clicked this picture of the Register while writing his name below theirs. And both your names are just above theirs, as you see it in the picture here."

"Oh, my God! What complications, man? And with amazing speed!" said Vijay with a surprise, as he thought his association with Jasmine too was getting wider publicity. But he decided to be on defensive.

"Look here guys, keep this in mind: you should not draw conclusions after seeing someone with somebody. They may be together for some reason, about some business, either their personal or social. But judging them wrong without verifying is immoral on our part."

With a small pause Vijay continued: "My dear son and daughter, by now you must have realised as to why I have not been open and avoided telling the truth. I know you would understand my mission but Mom would not. She would fantasise the improbable and hurt herself mentally and emotionally. I needed to protect her."

"Are you still going to see that lady, Dad?" interrupted Judith.

"See, we live in a civilised society Judy. Having done several sessions of counselling already, how can I withdraw from it now? Do you want me to tell that suffering lady that your Mummy is narrow-minded and taking objection to my helping her? If I say so, won't I damage Mummy's self-respect? Won't she be disgraced in Jasmine's eyes?" Said Vijay.

Vijay joined both his hands at his chest, like in prayer, and shaking them up and down said, "This is not the time to throw muck at one another, Sanjay and Judy. We have more serious problem at our doorstep. We need to investigate Mom thoroughly with medical check-ups. No one knows how that scorpion sneaks into the house these days."

"Yes Dad, I am taking an appointment with the physician tomorrow. Let's hope nothing serious shrouds over Mom." said Sanjay.

When they returned home, Maria was burning with fever again.

XXIV

By and large Vijay took a holiday from evening walks on Sundays. But today he couldn't wait for Monday. Based on revelations at the Church garden, he wished to take counsel from Jasmine, conversely this time!

"I need to meet you urgently. Let me know immediately when and where."

Vijay checked the mobile if the ticks had turned blue, but in vain. He checked it every five minutes and finally gave up, presuming that Jasmine must have gone out, somewhere.

The next day afternoon Jasmine replied:

"Not well…"

"What's up?"

"Menses…severe pain…unbearable."

"Oh, sorry…"

"Need you close...I'll feel better."

"Serious! – Maria's not well."

"OMG…shall I come?"

"No way…it will be messier!"

"Shut up…"

"Sanjay is checking Travel Insurance docs to determine liability."

"Forget the liability. Just admit her to the Hospital. Keep me posted."

Private and paid medical services in Australia cost astronomically high compared to India.

"Dad, I'm just going through your Travel Insurance Papers, fine-printed terms and conditions in particular… Oh, I see, you're insured for OPD also. So let's take Mom to our family clinic for checking." Sanjay said with some relief.

The next day Sanjay and Vijay took Maria to Casualty section of the Sir John Monash Private Hospital. He took along with him all the travel insurance papers including passports and visas, etc.

Dr. Anand Desai, a recent young and energetic Indian immigrant, had shot up to fame for his accurate diagnosis in the City of Monash, located in Clayton suburb,19 km south-east of Melbourne's central business district.

During physical check-up Dr. Desai went through the vital signs on the case paper the nurse had noted and asked, "Mrs. D'Souza do you get fever with chills?"

"Yes."

"Do you feel weak and dizzy?"

"Yes."

"Do you feel hungry?"

"No."

Dr. Desai recommended some crucial blood tests. The nurse in the Pathology took Maria's blood samples and requested the foursome to wait in the lobby for results.

Vijay walked towards the payment counter pretending to watch around the workings of the OPD and casually took out his mobile.

'At John Monash Pvt. Hospital…

Dr. Anand Desai recommended blood tests…

Awaiting results…

It may take an hour or so.

Hope nothing's serious with her.' V

'I too pray for her good health. Let me know the results and you take care.' J

Vijay felt happy that Jasmine, being from the medical field, was kept informed.

Little over an hour and a nurse approached Sanjay and signalled him toward doctor's room. Vijay also followed him gesticulating Judith to remain with Maria.

Dr. Desai said, "I see some weird and irregular strains in blood samples. I'm recommending Mrs. D'Souza to the Oncology Department on the first floor. Dr. Jacob Daniels is the Onco Physician and Dr. David McCollum is Onco Surgeon. That is a very proficient and famous pair of Super-Specialists in this part of the world.

With the mention of Oncology Vijay and Sanjay looked at each other's face. They mentally concluded that it was something to do with the Scorpion.

Dr. Daniels shuffled through blood reports and suggested some more detailed tests and said, "You'll get the results tomorrow. Now you can go home and bring Mrs. D'Souza tomorrow evening for further check-up. Perhaps she may require hospitalization."

Vijay and Sanjay nodded their heads with depressing feelings and came out of Doctor's consulting room.

"Dad, you all take these car keys and be seated in the car. I'll drop Mediclaim papers in the office for processing," said Sanjay in a dejected mood.

Sanjay drove the car out of the parking lot. Maria rested her head behind on the headrest of the car and pretended to sleep by closing her eyes in order to rob their conversation, in case they discussed the nature of her illness. No one spoke a word till they reached home. Their silence spoke a thousand words, words which no one was prepared to hear.

Nicky and Nilufer were anxiously waiting for them. "What happened Sanju is everything alright with Mummy?" inquired Nilufer.

"We hope nothing is serious with Mom. We'll get the blood reports tomorrow and Dr. Daniels has called again tomorrow evening. By that time you all will be half way home," said Sanjay to defuse everyone's depressed mood.

"Brother, I don't feel like going back to India leaving Mamma in this condition," said Judith.

"Don't be silly, we are here to take care of Mom. Nicky has to report to work as he is due for his Managerial post," said Sanjay patting Judith's shoulder as an assurance.

During baby Ajay's Baptism party, people from Vasai living in Melbourne had known about Fernandes' departure to India. Even if one person knows the date, the news spreads like wildfire and people prepare small parcels as token of love to their dear ones back home. The travellers are prepared for this kind of Indian tradition, because they also follow the same norms while others go home.

Towards the evening Vasai Community people started to visit the D'Souza's with their parcels to be given to their respective relatives in Vasai. Charles and Samantha came, followed by Alex and Emily. Then Sabby and Scarlet with baby Bella arrived and then others.

Their Australian neighbours Keith and Camilla Brown had planned to give a small farewell barbeque party in honour of Sanjay's sister and brother-in-law. He brought in a large vessel of marinated lamb chops and lit the gas barbeque on the patio behind Sanjay's house.

The gents cheered with beer and scotch around the barbeque and ladies were served wine in the living room; none being aware that horrendous health calamity loomed over the D'Souza's!

Despite such a catastrophe, Vijay exhibited external serenity but internally he was deeply destabilized by Maria's ailment. It was his better-half's very life that was at stake! Without her he would lose his comprehensive identity in social milieu.

Although there were differences between Vijay and Maria, they couldn't live one day apart without each other. One may call it love, others,–possessiveness and still others,–jealousy and therefore over protectiveness! Unlike prewritten scripts in drama, here impromptu arguments and dialogues would be delivered ex-tempore by each actor in the family, depending on what role each one of them played in response to various relationships and situations. They would either be recalled from memory or reproduced later on.

At this point Vijay badly needed company of someone who would understand him; who would identify with his agonising self. And who would be ready to share with him his agony?

From all angles, from all sides, from all degrees, from all latitude and altitude, the pointer directed at no one else but Jasmine.

His was a Platonic love alright but her's might not have been equally so; hers perhaps could be romantic or sexual. And that was the clash of cultures which Vijay wished to resolve before committing himself into any relationship!

He remembered in one of their arguments Jasmine had said: "According to me, there is no such a thing called Platonic Love. Either you have sensual desire or pretend you don't. By nature person generally cannot be free from sensual desire, unless he/she suppresses it for a sublime cause. That suppression is detrimental to mental and physical human growth. The ill effects of this factor are reflected in various psychological disorders."

*****

"Hey Sanju, are you all ready? I am already in front of your house," said Charles over mobile from his parked vehicle.

"Hi Charlie, come in…have some breakfast *'Yar'* (friend)," said Sanjay while putting his shirt on. "Judy, is the coffee ready? Please remove the croissants from the Micro, they must be warm enough."

"Can you see if Mamma is awake, Daddy?" knocked Judith on the door.

"Yeah…yeah…I'm just giving her a face wash," said Vijay from the bath.

"Brother, can Mom accompany us to the airport? Last night she was insisting on seeing us off." said Judith in a pleading manner.

"No my dear Sis…the doctor said to keep her in secluded place and avoid all kinds of infection-prone areas. What's the difference if she kisses good-bye here or at the airport? It's the question of her health, Sis…" said Sanjay trying to make Judith understand.

Little Olivia couldn't be awakened. So, Nicky sprinkled a few drops of water on her face but in vain. Finally he lifted her in his arms and placed carefully on the hind seat of Charles's car. Judith hugged Mamma and bid her adieus.

Within an hour the D'Souza clan reached Melbourne Airport. Before the threesome Fernandes family proceeded to the check-in and immigration counters, tearful Hugs and embraces galore were exchanged among them.

*****

As the evening approached anxiety rode high on Vijay's and Sanjay's minds. The scene was, doctors in the consulting room on the second floor of Sir John Monash Private Hospital–Dr. Jacob Daniels, the Oncologist Physician and Dr. David McCollum, the Oncologist Surgeon. And in front of them were seated Mr. & Mrs. D'Souza and their son Sanjay, waiting for the pronouncement of Doctors' verdict.

“Sister Sophie, let Mrs. D’Souza lie on bed in the checking room please.” Said Dr. Daniels and continued with a grim face, “Well, the reports are not very encouraging, but we’ll do our best to arrest further growth.”

“Let me explain to you in medical terms,” said Dr. McCollum and continued, “Leukaemia is cancer of blood-forming tissues, including bone marrow. Many types exist such as acute lymphoblastic leukaemia, acute myeloid leukaemia and chronic lymphocytic leukaemia.”

“And hers is the last type – Chronic Lymphocytic Leukaemia,” said Dr. Daniels. “Many patients with slow-growing types of leukaemia don’t have symptoms. Rapidly growing types of leukaemia may cause symptoms that include fatigue, weight loss, frequent infections and easy bleeding or bruising, such as in Mrs. D’Souza’s type.” said Dr. Daniels honestly in rather cold blooded manner.

Dr. McCollum said, “Treatment is highly variable. For slow-growing leukaemias, treatment may include monitoring. But in your case, aggressive treatment includes chemotherapy, which is sometimes followed by radiation and stem-cell transplant.”

Vijay and Sanjay listened to the Doctors’ narrations looking at each other intermittently with saddened faces.

“We will have to start the treatment with Chemo immediately. Initially for a few days, Mrs. D’Souza will be kept in an isolation ward. We need to avoid infections, so you will be able to see her through the glass window. Later on we will move her to the common ward.” Dr. McCollum instructed the D’Souza’s.

As they got out of the Doctors' chamber, Vijay couldn't wait to break the news to Jasmine. He went to the 'Men's'.

"Detected Leukaemia…" V

"What…??? OMG…!!" J

The next moment Vijay put his mobile off, for he couldn't see anything on the screen with tearful eyes.

Sanjay waited for Dad outside 'Men's'. As both looked at each other they impulsively hugged tight and sobbed for a couple of minutes. They cried from within, their shoulders just shuddered. No one spoke a word. Their waves were on the same hertz. They released from the embrace and took out kerchiefs to wipe tears and nasal mucus.

"Sanjay, you get going…Nilufer and baby are alone at home. She must be worrying about Maria."

"Ok Dad, you take care and let us pray that Mom gets well soon." Said Sanjay and left for home.

The visiting D'Souza's were in the middle of the third month. Two weeks remained before they had to leave Australia. To be eligible for grant of another three months' visiting Visa, as per immigration rules, they had to remain at least one day out of Australia.

When problems crop up people recollect their friends and foes. Vijay suddenly remembered Bhupinder Singh, the Alibi.

"Hi Bhupinder Singh how are you? How is your family back home?" Vijay greeted Bhupinder through mobile.

"Oh, they are fine and I'm also good."

"Has extension of your work permit not expired yet?" asked Vijay.

"No *Saheb* (Sir). I followed your advice you gave me in the Park. Got promoted and my family will be joining me soon. I'm very happy, *Saheb*."

"I am not."

"Why, what happened, Sir?"

"Nothing much...but...wife not well..."

"Not well meaning? Not too much well or not little well?".

"She's got blood cancer...Leukaemia."

"Oh my God! Where is she?" said Bhupinder in disbelief.

"She's under treatment at Sir John Monash Private Hospital close by. She is in the isolated ward and no visitors allowed." Vijay warned in case he would plan to visit.

"Oh my...my...let me know if I can be of any help, Sir." .

"Listen Bhupinder, hardly two weeks left to go back to India and in such situation how can we go?"

"You don't have to Sir, apply for extension under medical grounds. Australians are very humane Sir and they consider such cases beyond anyone's control." Bhupinder said with confidence.

"OK Bhupinder, I'll get back to you later." Said Vijay and as he was putting the instrument in his pocket, the mobile rang.

"Dad...it's me. How's Mom doing?" asked Sanjay.

"I just had a look from the glass window. The Chemo is on and she is asleep. What can we do son? Why has it come upon us? I can't understand," said Vijay with thin and quivering voice.

"Yeah Dad, Nilu is crying ever since..." Sanjay broke down.

"Dad...go to the Canteen on the ground floor and eat something," said Sanjay.

"No...no...I don't feel like having anything."

"I will come after a while, Dad. Please Dad...take hold of yourself." Said Sanjay and put his mobile off.

Vijay sat on the couch in the lobby in front of the Isolated Ward, bent forward with his head held in both his hands.

Vijay felt a soft palm stroking his back gently and lovingly. He had already smelt Jasmine when she was twenty feet away. Therefore, he retained the same position he was in. Jasmine sat compactly at Vijay's left side.

"I understand your grief darling...Be brave and face life as it unfolds... I am with you in your hard times... Don't give up so easily...You are a counsellor and a strong man." Jasmine whispered slowly with disjointed phrases.

Vijay still remained in the same position for a while. Then lifting his head up he turned left. At that very moment Jasmine's lips touched his for a flash of a moment. This time Vijay felt good. He needed that warmth and loving concern at that time of tribulation. Jasmine was ever ready to offer it to him. He had no reaction to the impulsive occurrence as he looked at her blankly.

Jasmine asked Vijay with her eyes where Maria was? He showed his three fingers, meaning Room No. 3.

"Hey Dad, did you have something to eat?" said Sanjay taking Vijay by a sudden surprise.

"No...I'm not hungry."

"You have some snacks here," said Sanjay seeing a packet of sandwiches and a small bottle of coke lying on the couch.

"Yeah, that lady Jasmine Singh has come to visit Mom. Past half an hour she is in there. I wonder what she is up to. But nothing to worry, she is a professional nurse." said Vijay before Sanjay could ask any questions.

"Let me go and have a look. In the meantime please have the sandwich Dad."

Sanjay peeped through the glass and saw a tall Australian lady with a mask on her mouth was monitoring the IV fluid drops and talking to the hospital nurse.

Sanjay came back to where Vijay was sitting and said, "Dad, there is no Jasmine Singh in there."

"Oh, you mean she disappeared without saying anything?" said Vijay regretfully.

After a while Jasmine came out and stood near Sanjay still with her mask on.

Vijay looked up, "Oh, there you are. I thought you had left," said Vijay with wrinkles on his forehead.

Removing her mask Jasmine said, "How can I go without letting you know. The nurse and I were fixing the dribble of the IV flow," said Jasmine professionally.

Vijay stood up and said, "Sanjay, this is Lady Jasmine Singh. And Jasmine this is my son Sanjay."

"Hi, how do you do? I am Jasmine," said Jasmine jutting out her hand in front.

"Hi, how do you do? I'm Sanjay," Sanjay returned the greeting and they shook hands.

Sanjay was rather surprised to see this gentle and beautiful Australian lady, excellently refined against her Indian name 'Jasmine Singh'!

Magpie: The fragrance from that flower 'Jasmine' has spiritually scented the ambience of the floor, especially for you Vijay!

Shut up Magpie, This is not the time for your funny remarks. Now it's a question of life and death!

"Can I not get to see Mom? How is she doing Ms. Jasmine? Will she be alright, on her feet again?" Sanjay asked with filial concern.

"Look Mr. Sanjay, I just went through all the tests reports. I think you all should have brought her in much earlier. Both the Oncologists are experts in the field; they have started with a strong dose. But again it all depends how her body responds. The atmosphere has to be extremely sterile; in such condition the patient is highly volatile for infection. You come in tomorrow morning and we will meet the doctors together," said Jasmine with a smile.

"C'mon Dad…it's late and we can't stay here any longer. Since ours was a fresh admission they allowed us till now. Otherwise they vacate visitors at 6.30 pm. At 7 pm patients are served dinner. Am I right Ms. Jasmine?" Sanjay said.

"You are right Mr. Sanjay. But I will take Dad down to the Canteen to eat this sandwich. Otherwise, I know, he'll go hungry."

"No…no…I will not go home, I will stay on here in the Hospital," insisted Vijay.

"No one is allowed to stay here for the night, Dad. Only the patients and the staff; and in case, dead bodies!" said Sanjay with a serious tone.

“Oh…OK…I’ll drop him home…what Fulton Street is it?” Jasmine asked.

“504”, Sanjay said at the tip of his tongue.

“Bye Ms. Jasmine, nice to have met you; see you around,” said Sanjay as Vijay and Jasmine turned right to the Canteen and Sanjay exited the building.

This young lady seems to be very smart. In a short time she has studied Dad well enough to know his habits! Sanjay thought.

In the Canteen Jasmine moved around with ease of acquaintance as many staff helloed her and exchanged smiles.

“You seem to be very popular in this place Jasmine,” said Vijay.

“Actually, I forced myself to come here. I avoid this place. This place takes me back to horrendous memories, Vijay.”

“Why? What’s so special about this place?”

“This is where I met that skunk! He was some maintenance guy eyeing on me from my day one on the job. I worked for three years and left the job. I took up a break-duty in the Safeway chain of stores just to dodge the stalker. But that job was killing on me.”

“But then why did you get Married?” asked Vijay.

“One day this guy came along with some of his Aussie and Indian friends, well-dressed to impress my father. Though my father was very rigid and dictatorial, they managed to persuade him like they do in India. Himmat Singh gave away his daughter in wedding to Jim. Once he decided something he would not retract. I had no choice but to succumb to Daddy's pressure. I have been victimised."

Jasmine further continued, "Remember the second time you came to my house and I told you how this brute treated me? Later on he went further and forced me to go on drugs. He even encouraged his friends to abuse me."

"What?" exclaimed Vijay.

"He drained both our salaries. Within a couple of months I filed my papers and returned to my parents. It has taken me three years to close that chapter." Jasmine said as tears rolled down her cheeks.

She continued further, "In society when people inquire with me about Jim, I say he is on Company sponsored study tour. What else can I say? I have to stand respectable in the society anyway."

"How is he doing these days, any news?" inquired Vijay.

"His relatives meet me sometimes at the Mall. They say he is sinking."

"Don't you want to see him for the last time, perchance?" Vijay touched on very sensitive issue.

"Vijay, love is nothing but a transient feeling, which keeps on fading with time and with one's mood. If your so called loved one does not care anymore about you or leaves you, be patient, time will wash away aches and sadness. One needs to be practical in life, never to exaggerate the beauty and sweetness of falling in love and never to exaggerate the sadness of falling out of love. You need to be indifferent like I am right now," said Jasmine firmly.

"Again Mr. D'Souza," she continued, "physical union does not necessarily mean there is love and affection. It can be used purely for the release of natural urge that gives pleasure feeling to one's body. But when the union is correlated with true emotive love, the physical and spiritual union culminates into a spiritual reality, the summit of existence of human beings. So, for me Jim is a non-existing entity. Whether he is alive or dead, does not make any difference to my being alive and my life ahead." Jasmine said uninterruptedly.

"And please Mr. D'Souza, do not think that I fell in love with you for sex or for any other selfish motive. It is for a simple reason that you are genuine and transparent. I do not wish to rob the pleasure and comfort of your family members from you. But I want to make it more substantive and enjoyable for all of us if you include me in." said Jasmine with invigorated zest.

"But why are you giving me this lecture?" said Vijay in a pathetic tone.

"Two and a half months back I did not know you from Adams. But at the first encounter in the Princess Highway Reserve Park, when I came to know that you were from India, Indian blood in my arteries sprang up like the crude in Arabian Desert. I felt some connection between us. I dared to tell you lies that I was from Bombay, just because I wanted to identify myself as an Indian. At that time I was experiencing a desert of my life worse than the Sahara." said Jasmine without a pause.

She was bent on giving Vijay a piece of her mind: "Vijay, you deserve the best in life, but you have become a victim of your Indian culture and traditions. You can't take a single step or breathe without consciously or unconsciously taking approval from your people and their unwritten laws! Is that life? Let loose, be free and be liberated, you don't need to be religious or scrupulous to do just that!"

"Jasmine, it's getting late, shall we go?" asked Vijay.

"Just be seated here Vijay, I will take one last round at Maria and see how she is doing. I would love to take you with me but they will not allow you at this time of the night. The guards have changed since I left."

Vijay's mind was in turmoil. Not only that he did not want to reflect on whatever Jasmine said but he wished he had not heard it at all!

Magpie: After listening to Jasmine's discourse, you have become dumbfounded. You are caught in a whirlwind of your own creation, spinning 380 degrees with great speed. You are being tossed around. At times being lifted high up into the air and at others, being suddenly dropped on an island, all alone! You started trembling and shivering. It was a tug of war for you–being pulled between Maria's illness and Jasmine's past agonising life-story.

XXVI

Vijay's mobile rang...

"Tell me Sanju..."

"Dad, if that Lady is gone, I'm coming to pick you up?"

"Don't worry Sanju. Jasmine is dropping me home. We'll be there in a minute."

"There we are...504, Fulton...I hope they are still awake." said Jasmine while parking her car in front of Sanjay's house.

"How can they retire when the Matriarch is in the Hospital and the Patriarch has not yet arrived home?" said Vijay as he got out of the car.

As Sanjay saw them both stepping up the stairs he opened the main door for them and said, "Come...come... welcome to our house Ms. Jasmine. Niluuu, we have a guest...This is Ms. Jasmine and Jasmine this is my wife Nilufer." Sanjay introduced both of them very briefly.

"How's Mummy Dad? Is she responding to the medication?" asked Sanjay.

Before Vijay could say anything, Jasmine said, “It’s too early to talk about results. The effects of Chemo won’t be noticed yet. Let three months of treatment go through.”

“When can we get Mummy home, Jasmine?” asked Nilufer.

“Again, it all depends on how her body responds to the treatment. Why are you so much in a hurry? Your parents can get extension of their visiting Visas on medical grounds.” said Jasmine to diffuse their anxiety.

“That way Sanju has already informed his office about his Mom’s condition that he would sometimes need time-off to attend to her illness.” said Nilufer to safeguard her husband.

Sanjay intervened and said, “But the day after tomorrow I am scheduled to be in Sydney for two days’ PPT presentation to a group coming from Poland for a business deal. I’m in a fix; I don’t know how to manage with this situation out of the blues!”

“Listen guys, no one has to be worried about Maria. I am able to take care of her and I will stay there the whole day,” said Vijay.

“It’s not the question of being there the whole day, but more importantly one must know what to do in case of emergency and know things and places to run around! Dad, do you know any of the departments there?” said Sanjay with a raised voice.

“Mr. Sanjay, you don’t have to get so excited. I am there to take care of your mother. Whether or not you appoint me as an official care-taker Nurse, I am ready to give my free services just for your Dad and his wife Maria and your family!” said Jasmine with a spirited voice.

For a second everyone in the living room became quiet. Nursing services don't go cheap in Australia and this dame was offering her services free of cost!?

Having a woman's alertness, Nilufer immediately wondered about Jasmine's ulterior motive. But at that moment of her lactating baby, she did not have much choice but to accept any help that came from any quarters.

Initially, it was a day at a time that soon became a weekly routine. Sanjay took Vijay to visit Maria in the mornings on his way to the Office. Jasmine came late morning but did a lot of running around, sponge-bathing Maria, giving her medication in time, talking to Doctors and following their advice. In the evenings Jasmine would drop Vijay at Sanjay's on her way home.

The grant of extra two months Visa was nearing completion. By this time Maria was left with little hair on her head. She wore a scarf at all times. Maria was scheduled for discharge soon. She longed to see baby Ajay after a long gap.

Very often Vijay and Jasmine sat in the lobby and chit-chatted about their families and other topics of interests to both.

On one such occasion Vijay asked, "You refused the money that Sanjay offered you for your services, so how do you manage your monthly expenditure, Jasmine?"

"Money is not everything in life, Vijay. It is only a means to an end. There's certain thing called love, social concern for the needy and understanding of international brotherhood. My father, Himmat Singh, had deposited a sizable amount of money in my name in the banks and company bonds. Plus my Mom gets her pension from Qantas, in addition to her Social Security and savings.

All put together and without any family liabilities, I am well-off to pay house, electricity and water taxes to the City Council Office and maintain myself and also save a little bit." said Jasmine with a gentle sweet smile.

"Don't you feel bored by yourself?"

"That's the reason I do that 'Casual' job at the Safeway's. But now I have a special reason to get up in the morning and get going during the day." said Jasmine while expanding her eyebrows.

"What reason?" questioned Vijay instantly.

"Well, time will tell…!" said Jasmine and got up from her seat to attend to Maria in Room No. 3.

Magpie: Ah…ha! I had warned you to be on your guards. The slithery snail moves at its own pace but it does! At first she won your sympathy, then your heart and now she has won your family's admiration and gratitude. You won't know what is in store for you!

Leave me alone Magpie. I am in the midst of a crisis and you have no work but to irritate me with your baseless allegations!

Magpie: Oh yeah? Allegations?…For whose cause are you separating me from your being, may I know? You think you are alone and can do anything by yourself. But let me tell you my friend, I am your 'well-formed conscience', and you cannot fool around me. I will always be with you; not only like a mirror which reflects the image fallen on it, but a layer of a mercury which analyses the real you.

With this prompt suggestion Vijay came to his senses. He remembered Maria and rushed to her bedside. But he immediately froze as he saw Jasmine giving Maria a sponge bath. He could have entered in there if any

Doctor were present with Maria. But with Jasmine being there, his Indian mindset could not undervalue Jasmine's physical reverence vis-à-vis Maria's uncovered body!

One day Vijay and Jasmine were seated in the lobby on the second floor of the hospital, and a message jingled on her mobile:

"Sad news…Jim's no..mo…"

"What?...what happened?"

"Dunn…knu…"

"When's funeral?"

"Club members pooled...direct cremation through Melbourne Funeral Services at Clayton."

"Thanks…"

"What's the matter Jasmine? What happened? Anything serious?" asked Vijay as he saw her face turning sombre while she exchanged mobile messages.

She just nodded her head and stared blank on the floor:

With Jim gone...one more chapter is over! Before him my father died, tomorrow my dear Mom will depart! And after that it'll be my turn. ...So what! Eventually everyone has to go from this world. No one is immortal, not even memories! 'Cause memories die too with the person. My love for Jim was innocent and pure, but it died early unnatural death. It died because of errors and betrayals. It died of maltreatment and wounds. It died of aimless living, disillusionment, arrogance and defilement. Jim acted with physical impulse but never with rationale. He just lived for the day and for himself. That was just carnal lust and no love. For the past five years I am starving and searching for love...but...

"I said what's the matter and you're not responding, Jasmine. What happened all of a sudden?" persisted Vijay.

"Things in my life happen suddenly, without forewarning. And that's why life is thrilling!" said Jasmine. "It's Jim…he is no more!"

"What? Your husband is no more? And you can say that so easily, without any remorse?" said Vijay with a surprise.

"So?…what do you expect me to do, scream and shout? Tell the whole world that my lawfully wedded husband is dead and gone? He was dead to me long back, Vijay! I have experienced 'living death' many a time in that short period. For him I was just a body, almost a dead corpse. For the past four years it did not make any difference to me whether he was alive or dead. So, why should it make now?" said Jasmine as a matter of fact.

Vijay was shocked at Jasmine's indifference and started to reflect: *What kind of a culture is this,* he thought. *People do not care for each other even when they are dead and gone! In India they mourn the dead, whether young or old, for days and months on end! Especially in Vasai, any funeral looks like tranquil gathering of thousands of people. Some attend it as a social obligation and others want to make sure that relatives and parishioners should attend their funeral in such big numbers. Though they will not be alive to witness the same! Isn't it a paradox of life?*

"Jasmine, I think we should pay a condolence visit to Jim's people," said Vijay innocently.

"Who people? He had no people! Who he had were all his druggist friends. I was the only normal relation he had, that too for a short while." said Jasmine despicably.

At this point Vijay thought there was no point in pursuing the matter with Jasmine on this subject. So, he changed the subject and said, "Jasmine, two weeks from now and we'll be out of here. You've been a tremendous help to us. We have been highly indebted to you and do not know how and when to repay it."

"Please Vijay, don't be so rude to me. I did it all for you and your family. By expressing gratitude, you are devaluing that beautiful relationship of love."

"Oh yeah…certainly…it was Maria's illness that brought you so close to my family. We'll find it difficult to part with you when Maria has got so used to you. But at the same time we want very much to go back to our motherland, where our roots are deep. And we wish to be buried in our homeland."

"Hold on Vijay, I have an idea. I know an Immigration Lawyer who can advise if you can be sponsored by Sanjay for a permanent residence," said Jasmine hopefully.

"Jasmine, I don't think Maria and I wish to stay here any longer. Certainly, the civic discipline, cleanliness and corruption-free administration attract us to live here permanently. But we would still prefer to live in a society that we have grown up with. Things and facilities are meant to give us comfort in living standard. But without proper mental disposition and value system they become worthless." said Vijay from his heart.

Magpie: Why are you putting on, Buddy? Are you serious you want to leave pleasant company of Jasmine in Melbourne? If not for Maria's illness, you would have gone back to India in the coffin or be buried here for sure! Who in India can dream of such clean life? Except for those corrupt politicians and government servants, who steal billions of Rupees from tax-payers money and live in luxurious life-style!

"Vijay, as we discussed with Dr. Daniels and Dr. McCollum, Maria should be discharged tomorrow morning. I checked with the Administration and confirmed that they have received the amount from the Mediclaim Department of the Insurer." Said Jasmine and continued, "Please tell Sanjay there is no need to stay back from work, we both can manage with the Ambulance."

"That would give us hardly two weeks to prepare for our departure," said Vijay with concern of no importance.

"Do not worry, I can go with you for last minute shopping if you would like," offered Jasmine her free services. "By the way," she further instructed Vijay, "please go to the Pathology Lab downstairs and give a blood sample for your diabetes. I have filled your form and spoken to the Sister-in-Charge there."

The next couple of days were very hectic for Jasmine. She arrived in the mornings at Sanjay's and completed routine medical chores for Maria. They had lunch together and took a little siesta. Sanjay had sanction from his boss to leave two hours early to attend to his ailing mother. After Jasmine would have done with Maria's routine, Sanjay could take Nilufer, Dad and Jasmine for shopping during early evenings.

"Sanju baba, why are you spending so much money on shopping? Are we obligated to take loads of stuff for our neighbours and relatives? Don't we get these things in India nowadays? Who's going to carry this weight? Plus Nicky and Judy have just gone with loads of food stuff and chocolates. So, don't you worry about shopping anymore!" pleaded Vijay.

"Exactly, I was going to say this myself. You may not carry huge bags filled with things for anyone outside your own family members. And yours is nucleus family, not a big gang!" Jasmine tried at a joke but no one laughed, for there was a serious point in what she said.

"Yeah, you're right Jasmine. Maria will be on a wheelchair. I should see to her comfort all throughout and not be worried about the luggage!" Vijay said to support Jasmine.

"Ok…ok…so we relax in the house and talk to darling Mom. Entertain her a little." Sanjay said, to close the argument.

XXVII

Seated in a wheelchair after porridge-n-toast breakfast, Maria suddenly brought up the topic of Home Nurse. "This Nurse Jasmine Singh by name sounds like Indian but looks and behaves like an Australian. Who is she and where is she from? Can anyone tell me?"

The three of them in the Living Room were taken aback with Maria's unwarranted question and started looking at each other's faces. Who would dare endeavour a fitting answer that would not generate another question from Maria, was the real knack of argument with her?

Vijay virtually was not a candidate to know anything about this young beautiful and active nurse, so he had to keep his mouth shut! Nilufer saw this dame only after Mom was hospitalized. Therefore, all eyes pointed at Sanjay.

"Mom, we hired her services from the Home Nurses Guild pool to take special care of you. You know Nilu is tied up with the baby and I have to attend my duty.

After enquiries we found out that she is from an Indo-Australian mixed lineage." said Sanjay to satisfy Maria.

"What does that mean...?" Maria.

"Simply put her Father is an Indian and her Mother an Australian. They fell in love and got married in the Church," added Vijay.

"But she is a sweet lady, taking good care of me lovingly. She is not like the regular nurses who rush to complete their job without any feelings for the patient," said Maria in appreciation of Jasmine.

With this statement from Maria, Vijay's heart puffed-up with ultimate delight. But he could not afford to reflect it out on his façade.

The word had spread to the Vasai East Indian Community that Maria was brought home and the visiting parents were to fly home soon. Many of the families and Sanjay's Goan, Mangalorean Christian and non-Christian friends living in Melbourne came to visit the D'Souza's in the evenings.

On one such evening Charles and Samantha came to visit the D'Souza's. Charles was always ready to help Sanjay for any odd jobs and vice-versa.

"Sanjay, our Commune wants to host a parting get-together for Mom and Dad. When do you think is the best day and time?" asked Charles.

"Charlie, tell them I appreciate the gesture but with the nature of Mom's illness it would look a little odd."

"We know the gravity of the situation, but we are not going to dance and make merry like Christmas or New Year Party."

"Ok, let me think it over. I will confirm this evening… whatever," said Sanjay not to refuse the Commune's good gesture.

Sanjay consulted with Dad, Nilu and also with Judith and Nicky in Vasai. They all agreed in order to liven-up Maria's spirit, at a low profile though.

It was a barbeque party and as usual neighbours Keith and Camilla Brown had geared up for the event. As the guests started to arrive, the gents were directed to the Patio around the Grill and the ladies were accommodated in the living room.

When a sizable crowd had gathered, Sanjay called gents in the hall with their glasses in hand to raise a vote of thanks:

"Hi guys, in life we face good times and bad. Without the bad, we will not know the value of good ones. Very often the bad ones are a blessing in disguise. Like steroids they boost our spirit to accept the challenges and come out a winner. Only good times would make our life boring and monotonous. So we thank God for both that keep us going with a balance.

I must appreciate and thank each one of you for having played your part to make my parents' holidays a pleasant experience here in Melbourne. As all of you must have noticed already, Mr. Keith and Mrs. Camilla Brown are not our neighbours but truly our extended family (claps). They are ever ready for us 24x7 and we for them. When one of our families is out of Melbourne, we housesit each other's premises. This, I am convinced, is a real integration of cultures.

Dear friends, I would like to single out those who have helped my Mother in her illness. Your 'Get-Well' cards and floral bouquets certainly lifted her emotional state, to bear the pain that she is going through. We solicit your prayers and best wishes for her quick recovery.

It can never ever be disputed that all our parents are the most wonderful people on earth. First of all they gave us our life! Then through their sacrifices and hard work, they brought us up, educated us and finally helped us land in this beautiful adventurous land for our better future prospects. Many times they have curtailed their needs and enjoyable moments back home for our sake, which we will never be aware of. God bless them always! (claps and hurray's).

By calling them here on holidays most of us try to kill three birds in one shot. One is to give them an experience of mesmerising beauty of Australia; secondly to show them that we live a better and more comfortable life here than back home; and thirdly, but most importantly, to baby-sit our kids, which otherwise would cost one job. So, it's happy ending that both the parties are benefitted! (claps and wows and woos!)

One person I wish to specially thank is Lady Jennifer alias Ms. Jasmine Singh. Briefly – her father was an Indian immigrant, late Himmat Singh from Punjab and mother an Aussie–Jessica Smith. Back home we have inter-caste, inter-religious, inter-ethnic marriages but this was in true sense an inter-national marriage! (Laughs and claps).

Ms. Jasmine Singh did an excellent job of nursing on my Mom, whom Mom says she had already started missing a week before departure. We offered her compensation for her hours with Mom but she refused. So, as a token of our gratitude and love I request Dad to present this small gift to Jasmine on behalf of my Mom and all present here."

Vijay got up from his chair apparent reluctance, took the package from Sanjay and presented it to Jasmine saying, "A very big thank you, Ms. Jasmine." Everyone in the hall clapped and wondered what gift was in the box.

Jasmine very delicately undid the wraps and lifted the top that to the amazement of the guests exposed sparkling set of Swarovski bracelets. There were wows and woos galore, as the box went from one lady to another.

Jasmine being an eloquent speaker, grabbed the mike from Sanjay and started her discourse:

"Excuse me Ladies and Gentlemen, I am speaking without being asked to, but I feel it is necessary.

The country of your choice, Australia, is a great nation. I am her proud citizen as you all should be. Comparisons are odious, but India is no less great, for its seven thousand years of history and culture. My other half is proud of India too!

From day one I simply fell in love with the D'Souza family. The past two and a half months seem like two and a half days to me! Didn't realize how time passed.

Culturally there is a vast difference between Australians and Indian Diaspora. Since both blood streams run through me, I can talk on both authoritatively.

What I did for Maria was part of love for my Indian family. My father had a massive heart attack and there wasn't any chance to serve him in the hospital. So, here I had an opportunity to use my talents in remembrance of my Dad.

Indian joint family is very conducive for children to grow up with the influence of social and religious cultures. The age-old values teach them many things that come of use in later life as adults.

Whereas, in Australia due to affluence and individualistic attitude, people have become self-centred; they have lost the sense of family as a unit; the families are breaking down; community living and interaction has become scarce; couples are getting married with Divorce Insurance papers in hand! No one knows where it is all going to end and what the future holds for generations to come."

There was a pin-drop silence in the living-room and all faces looked in deep thought as Jasmine spoke.

Many minds were in turmoil, questioning whether they and their children too are getting into the same rut as Australians. Some of them seriously introspected their way of life in the newfound land. Maria and a few ladies looked at Scarlet because of her anglicized mannerism.

Jasmine's eyes filled with tears:

"I thank the D'Souza family for accepting my humble services and also for this beautiful gift. These bracelets will speak volumes of the love Indians have among themselves. The sparkles will keep memories of this family in particular and generally of all you dear friends, ever glowing in my mind. They have in fact tied my hands to the Indian culture on Australian soil. Thank you Maria and Vijay, thank you Sanjay and Nilufer and sweetie-pie Ajay."

With this unexpected eloquence, all were quietened; but Sanjay brought in the party mood by telling gents to move towards the patio for drinks and barbeque. The ladies had already opened their chatter-boxes, some sipping Champagne and others holding beer glasses.

Vasaikars in Melbourne had one more occasion to mingle and exchange news and views. Many assured Maria of their prayers for her quick recovery while others tickled and smiled at little baby Ajay.

The party ended on a happy note with tipsy gents singing, "They're a jolly good fellas, they are……and socio all of us."

With the last guest gone, it took the D'Souza's quite some time to clean up the area at which Jasmine too gave a helping hand.

At the very end Jasmine bid everyone good night with a hug and a kiss and requested Vijay to walk her to the car.

"Vijay, within two days you will be gone, but I will miss you the most. I will find it hard to pass my day without you and Maria around. It's been ages since we had heart-to-heart talk, Vijay."

"I know, Maria's illness kept all of us busy round the clock. Jasmine, we too will miss you a lot. You have been a great help to Maria, Jasmine."

"Vijay why don't you take a morning walk tomorrow and come to my house? We will have breakfast together and later come here to do Maria's routine," said Jasmine not expecting 'a no' from Vijay.

"That's a good idea, Jasmine!" said Vijay while opening the car door for her.

"Good night darling…" said Jasmine as she kissed Vijay on cheeks.

Jasmine got in the car and slowly drove away, as if her vehicle too did not wish to part with Vijay's company.

Vijay stood there like a statue until he could see the car take a left turn and become invisible.

XXVIII

It was a pleasant and cool morning the next day. Jasmine had kept the door partly open as usual. As she heard Vijay's footsteps on the wooden stairs at the entrance, Jasmine opened the door fully and welcomed Vijay and hand-signalled him to take seat on the couch.

"I am tired Jasmine!" Vijay said with a long sigh whilst sitting on the couch. He saw a letter pad on the Coffee table and asked Jasmine what she was busy writing about.

"Nothing dear, that is just a part of my diary," said Jasmine to sidetrack his mind from there and continued: "What are you tired of, dear?"

"I am tired of life!" he said.

"Why are you so depressed when all of us are around to take care of Maria?"

"It's not Maria's illness alone, dear Jasmine."

"Then what else is it?"

"It's a question of life! What is life? Why is it so complicated? Why is there so much suffering in the world? Why is there so much inequality and disparity among people? I get mad, Jasmine, when I start to think on these vital life issues!" said Vijay with exasperation.

"Don't be so down Vijay darling." Jasmine sat on the couch almost clinging to his body. She turned his head with her left hand towards her and said: "Look into my eyes, Vijay. What do you see in them?"

"Your blue and beautiful eyes, what else?"

"Can't you see your image in my eyes?"

"Oh yeah, that's right," agreed Vijay readily.

"So, you see, I have already captured you in my eyes and preserved you in my heart, darling Vijay," said Jasmine in a seductive manner.

Instantly Vijay got mesmerised. He rested his head backward on the couch and looked at the ceiling impassively. The adrenaline enzyme spurted in his body. Jasmine took that gesture of his as a consent. Dopamine hormones had hit her central nervous system. Her whole Being got set on fire. The craving reached its summit. The next moment she raised herself on her knees on the sofa, placed her left leg across his right side and landed her juicy lips on his. Within seconds both were lips-locked in ecstasy. Vijay had no chance to decipher if what was happening was real or fantasy, good or bad, right or wrong, moral or immoral. But the pleasure was unimaginable, irresistible, irrefusable, inexpressible, unconquerable and unstoppable!

The smooching went on for quite some time. Vijay did not realise that he had a throbbing erection. Jasmine's charm kept Vijay's rationale centre numb with oral pleasure while his part below the belt gushed with blood.

Her bud was slowly swelling into a flower ready to host the Bee. Impulsively her hand unzipped his fly. She craftily adjusted her posture to gauge his response. She saw him in ultimate ecstasy, floating on seventh heaven.

The next moment, while in the clinging position, Jasmine laid herself on the Couch along with Vijay on top. As a natural animal instinct, now Vijay followed the rhythm, which increased vigorously for some time. At the end of it there was a shudder, a jolt and a deep thrust, thunder and lightning of an ultimate union…Bee emptied its nectar into the hive. A male had gifted his loving memento to the female.

Once the ultimate gratification reached its climax, the muscles relaxed gradually and the speed of passionate groans and strong hisses of human bellows calmed down little by little. The next half hour was the most relaxing interlude for both Vijay and Jasmine which was missing in their individual capacity for quite a long period of time. Both were in oblivion, an ether world. There was calm after the storm!

All of a sudden, Jasmine was awakened from her rapturous state by a mobile call: "Jasmine, Mummy is waiting for you, are you coming?" said Nilufer from the other end.

"Oh yeah…sure...I had a headache in the middle of the night and I woke up late this morning. I should be there soon…give me fifteen minutes please." said Jasmine apologetically, telling a white lie.

"No problem, Jasmine; take your time…but we're worried about Daddy," said Nilufer.

"Why? What happened to him?" asked Jasmine.

"He's gone for his morning walk but hasn't returned so far...we are worried about him that he may get lost somewhere," said Nilufer with anxiety.

"No my dear...he can't get lost after so many months in Clayton. Perhaps he may have gone to a Mall to buy some last minute picks."

Jasmine heard Vijay started to snore and she lifted his right hand from top of her breasts and slowly relieved herself from his cuddle. She went to the wash room; washed and dressed herself up. After coming out she clicked Vijay's picture with her mobile camera in the position he was laying on the couch. She woke him up. Vijay got up with a jolt wondering which planet he was on! He stood up.

Hugging him once again Jasmine said, "Viju darling, I am the happiest person on earth today. I have been yearning for this LOVE experience since my adult life. My desire for a person I loved from the depths of my heart has for the first time culminated into a physical union. Sorry darling if I have taken the liberty to love you but I needed it. I will forever be grateful to you for it."

"Nilufer called and they are waiting for me. I'll get going in my car. Nilu said you had gone for a walk and they are worried about your whereabouts. Let us keep it that way. You please come walking so they should not think we were together. Go to some Mall on the way. Just pull the door locked as you leave the house," said Jasmine and left her house in rush to attend to Maria.

Vijay could not make out head or tail of what was happening around. He shook himself to come to his senses and know which place in Melbourne he was at. He thought the occurrence was an exhilarating experience in many years, just like the one he had with Maria after marriage.

Vijay then went to the washroom, cleaned himself and came out fresh. He tried to unwind the past one hour's episode but that part of his memory was temporarily gone into 'sleep mode'. His mind-screen was blurred. He sat on the dining chair and held his head between his hands supported by elbows on the dining table top.

Magpie: Didn't I tell in the beginning itself to be careful from this lady? I had warned you to watch your move or else you might get into deep shit. And now you are right there! D..e..e..p s..h..i..t!

I don't know what happened to me...I just became submissive and animated at the same time.

Magpie: Didn't she tell you to look into her eyes? And that was the trick. She put you under her spell and you could never resist it.

But I did not do anything to her sexually because that would be adulterous!

Magpie: Exactly, in other words, she made you sensually numb and she raped you. This is what happens in here. Here females take the lead because upper class males are more interested in cricket and footie and the rest drown themselves in alcohol or drugs.

What do you suggest I should do now?

Magpie: I have been always pinching you whenever you were about to falter but you turned a deaf ear. This dame had challenged you right from the beginning. Remember your first visit in this house when she saw you naked in the bath? Didn't she say if you had anything more special than a normal male? She said that both of you were married and that you both had seen your partners' bodies inside out. That was the process of taming you! Now you decide your own fate. You can become like an Australian!

What you mean Australian? All Australians are not like this?

Magpie: But you could become one. Settle down here; resemble a Magpie with two colours, black and white!

That night was horrible for Vijay. He could hardly get a wink's sleep: The journey ahead with luggage and Maria on the wheelchair...almost five months' comfortable and enjoyable routine had come to end...the pleasant company of Jasmine that he was going to miss...and above all the unpardonable blunder that occurred on the last day of his stay...were all churning in his mind.

The morals and principles that he stood for in his whole life became hollow and futile in an hour's pleasure time. These thoughts spun Vijay's mind and body from left to right and from right to left alternatively. He did not sleep until Sanjay knocked on his door early morning to freshen up and get going to the airport.

Hardest part of living together is parting from it. Charles as usual was there to help Sanjay with the bags and taking Maria and Vijay to Melbourne Airport. Jasmine, Nilufer and even baby Ajay were at the airport to bid goodbye to the Senior D'Souza's.

Jasmine took Vijay aside and slid an envelope in his pocket. She warned him not to open the letter until one and half months had passed after his arrival in India. And Vijay promised to obey her command.

There came an announcement to board the flight to Mumbai. Maria was on a wheelchair with an escort. The parting of the D'Souza's was very tearful for everyone.

XXIX

Nicky and Judith with baby Olivia had arrived at Mumbai airport to receive Daddy and Mummy much before time.

In the last week of May every year the East Indian Community living in Sahar Village area, where the Schhatrapati Shivaji International Airport is located, celebrate Annual Feast of The Cross situated in front of T2 Terminal by reciting prayers and singing hymns.

The Central Government of India acquired thousands of acres of agricultural land from the East Indian Catholic people of Sahar village and expanded the international airport which originally was at Santacruz. As a remembrance of their inheritance of the land, the Catholic Community people have retained The Cross, maintain it and venerate it with an annual religious function.

As soon as Judith and Nicky spotted Maria on the wheelchair with an escort and Vijay walking beside her, exit the Baggage clearance area, they waved their hands to call attention. Eyes met eyes. Judith and Nicky rushed to the opening of railing barricade and gave them a warm welcome with hugs and kisses.

"How have you been Mamma, we missed you and worried about you too." Judith said with tears in her eyes.

"I feel better now Judy. I'll be alright once we are in our own house at Vasai," said Maria with confidence.

Just about that time a procession of East Indian Community people passed by offering people steamed *'Chana'* (grams-chick beans) and soft drinks. The ladies were beautifully dressed in their *'Loogda'* (ethnic red sari) and gold ornaments. The gents were well dressed and children dressed in their First Communion white gowns and dresses looked like little fairies and angels. The religious part being over in front of the antique Holy Cross, now they sang wedding songs on the beat of the '*Ghumat*'. (an earthen rhythm instrument). The multi-ethnic multi-religious and multi-lingual crowd at the arrival lounge of T2 was enchanted with this surprise show of East Indian people, the original land owners on which the biggest and most busy Airport Terminal in India stood proudly.

Within an hour and half the entourage was in Vasai. Vijay and Maria did not take much time to settle in the house. Nicky and Judith had kept the house spic-n-span, as if it was not unused for several months.

Nicky had already taken an appointment with an Oncologist at the Tata Memorial Hospital in Mumbai. The next day both Judith and he went with loads of reports brought from Sir John Monash Hospital in Melbourne and met the Doctor. Dr. Shah went through the documents for almost half hour and shook his head in the negative. Nicky and Judith looked at each other.

“Doctor, can we get mother here for check up?” asked Judith.

“There isn’t much left to be checked now. She is your guest for some time to come. You all should get mentally prepared and give her palliative care. What she needs most is attention, love and care,” said Dr. Shah, the Oncologist.

Coming back home from Mumbai Judith and Nicky decided not to let father know what the Doctor said about mother, lest he broke down.

“Hi Mom, how are you feeling,” asked Judith as she entered Maria’s bedroom. Maria did not say a word but looked at Judith disinterestedly.

“Mamma darling, how are you feeling? Tell me what is happening to you? What do you want, your wish is our command, Mamma,” said Judith while stroking her left hand over Maria’s forehead. Maria just shook her head in the negative.

At that moment Vijay entered the room and asked, “So Judy, what did the Doctors say about Mummy?”

“Yeah Dad, Dr. Shah is a well-known doctor in Mumbai and he said to continue with the same medication for a couple of weeks,” said Judith as a matter of fact.

“But since you left in the morning she did not get up from the bed. She just took half a cup of soup at 10 O’clock. May be due to travelling exertion and lack of sleep, Mom must have taken to bed,” concluded Vijay.

No one suspected that Maria had gone to bed, never to get up on her feet again.

Vijay kept himself busy taking care of Maria day in and day out. He would ferment Maria’s hands and legs with warm or cold water as it soothed her. He would be extraordinarily alert even if Maria moved her eyelids in sleep. From time to time he would help Judith when she sponge-bathed Maria.

Although physically Vijay was at home, very often mentally he would be in Clayton or day-dreaming. He had an incurable infection. On the last day of his stay in Melbourne, he was infected by the 'love-bug'! There isn't any remedy for this infection. It surely takes the wicket, whether strong or weak, when one is bowled a googly.

Sanjay and Nilufer called every day evening on IMO that facilitated live conversation from both ends. Even Jasmine called on IMO intermittently. But for personal conversation Vijay and Jasmine used WhatsApp messaging system, as and when privacy made it possible for them.

'Hi, how's Maria?' Jasmine.

'She hasn't got up from bed ever since we have come back.'

'I know, for past one week you have been telling me the same thing, Vijay.'

'Then what else to say?'

'Let's chat something about us, Vijay.'

'What about us?'

'Whatever...'

'C'mon Jasmine, Maria is ill and you're taking it so lightly?'

'Precisely so! Vijay, you must keep in mind that one day all have to die. No one is immortal. I'm just trying to keep your spirits up. That should help you restrain yourself in case you have to face the unexpected.'

'Oh, ok. How are you?'

'Not well…missing you a lot.'

'Again you're coming on same track.'

'Can't help it Viju. I feel lonely ever since you two left.'

'We didn't come on PR!'

'Wish you had…come again after Maria gets well.'

'Oh, I have to go…got to jot down her temperature on the chart.'

'Don't go to her isolated room without a mask…and don't let many relatives visit her.'

'Ok…bye…Jasmine.'

Day by day Maria was sinking. Nicky and Judith were updating Sanjay every day on IMO. But they could not tell what Dr. Shah had said in Vijay's presence. So, one day Judith called Sanjay from her house.

"Hi Sanju…Mom is not well…she is sinking."

"Why have you kept her home? Why don't you move her to the Hospital?" said Sanjay irately.

"Bro, when I asked Dr. Shah from Tata Hospital if he would check Mom physically, you know what he said after going through all the medical reports? He said, "there is nothing left to check now. She will be your guest for some time to come." He further said, "we all should get mentally prepared and give her palliative care. What she needs most at this time is attention, love and care."

"Then why didn't you tell me this earlier?" Sanjay said irritably.

"Because Dad used to be around all the time and we didn't want to shake him up with the fact. Plus, we did not know it would happen so quickly," explained Judith.

"Ok, in that case I would have to get prepared for a trip home," said Sanjay in a soft voice while his hard disk spun. He further added, "It would be rather difficult for Nilufer though. She has been called before time to replace a colleague who went on an emergency leave. The Company has agreed to pay for Ajay's Crèche (baby care centre) bill."

"Whatever it is, keep your boss informed for minimum ten days' leave as imminent emergency leave for yourself."

"I would also check with Jasmine if she would be willing to give company to Nilufer at least for the nights," said Sanjay.

"That would be a great idea; keep Jasmine also informed about the impending calamity on the D'Souza family," said Judith as a matter of etiquette.

"Ok…I'll do that; you take care of Mom and dad too."

One morning Vijay went to Maria's secluded room at six in the morning, as was his usual practice.

"Good Morning darling Maria...Hope you are feeling better today..." said Vijay and placed his palm on her forehead as usual. But this time he felt her cold. He tried to shake her head by holding on to her chin... but no response. He thought the game was over. Instantly he rushed out of the room...picked the mobile and called Judith.

"Judy...Judy...my Maria is gone..." Vijay howled on the mobile. "I have lost...she has left me alone...!"

"Dad, don't shout...you can't be sure. We have to call the local doctor to confirm. I will call Dr. Patil immediately," Judith said under pressure.

Nicky and Nilufer came with GP Dr. Patil. At first he checked her pulse on the wrist, heartbeat on the chest with stethoscope and finally opened and closed the eyelids. Then he declared: "Mrs. Maria Vijay D'Souza is dead." Cause: 'Death Due To Cardiac Failure'.

A person or an animal cannot die unless and until his heart stops functioning. But to avoid legal implications physicians have devised this general medico-legal indemnity, by which they avoid specifying which disease actually caused stoppage of the heart.

Judith phoned Sanjay instantly and broke the sad news. He said it would take him minimum 15 to 20 hours to arrive and they couldn't possibly keep the body at home. So, they moved the corpse to the Mortuary at Cardinal Gracias Memorial Hospital in Vasai.

Vijay in his capacity could only inform Jasmine in case no one bothered to.

'My Maria is no more'.

'Sorry...got the news from Sanjay'.

The message about Maria's demise spread all over Vasai thru WhatsApp and phone calls. The funeral time was to be fixed as per Sanjay's ETA at Mumbai Airport, which was next day morning. As Sanjay was already airborne on his way home, they fixed the funeral time at 4.30 in the evening the next day.

Vijay, Nicky and other relatives sat in the veranda in a mournful manner. Friends and relatives and even general public started coming to offer condolence to the bereaved family members.

Gabby and other relatives and friends gave Nicky a helping hand in preparing for the funeral formalities, such as fixing funeral time with the Parish Priest, informing villagers, relatives and friends via social media and displaying notice boards at prominent places in the marketplace and Railway Stations, as well as sending letters to neighbouring parishes for public announcement at the Church service. They also had to arrange for the local Undertaker with the Hurst, wooden casket and funeral band.

This was a period of mourning and no immediate family member was interested in having formal meals that evening. But as per traditions neighbours and relatives gathered and prepared simple steam rice and Dal Curry. They had to request and persuade the D'Souza's to have their fill, lest they felt weak and could not withstand the onslaught of visitors and further events that would take place.

The next day morning, mortal remains of Late Mrs. Maria Vijay D'Souza were brought home in Hospital's Ambulance. The ladies gathered in their blacks, gave Maria's corpse a water bath cosmetically and dressed her up in typical East Indian red sari (*Loogda*), brocaded with gold and silver threadwork. They ornamented her with all her jewellery, a collection of more than twenty five years. She was set up in a well-decorated wooden casket and kept in the living room for *Darshan* (public viewing) and paying last respects.

People from neighbourhood and other parishes were lining up to pay their last respects. Towards noon sister Lizbeth and many relatives requested Vijay to have his simple afternoon meal but he refused to eat.

He went to his room, picked his mobile and texted Jasmine…

'My love Maria left me, Jasmine'.

'I am extremely sorry Vijay…we did our best…but couldn't save her at the end'.

'I need someone to hold me Jasmine…I'm falling apart…my other half is no more there for me…she's laying in the coffin…in front of me…she looks so beautiful in her East Indian red sari…but my Maria is not saying anything…not making eyes at me anymore …not getting upset with me…she has just shut her mouth and eyes too. You think she is angry with me, Jasmine? Then why didn't she tell me so? Why she took her own decision this time…and that too, to the extreme?...who can answer me? …can you Jasmine?'

'Vijay dear…right now I have no answers for your questions…life is a mystery…many saints and sages have come and gone but not defined what life is and our final destiny. Right now you don't think about it...take control of yourself…cry as much as you wish…but within your heart…don't make a public show...be a man!'

'Sanjay should be reaching there soon. I'm with Nilufer and baby Ajay. Your nephew Gabby will arrange to IMO the funeral rites for us. Be assured we are with you in spirit, Vijay.'

As Sanjay approached the house everyone was on their feet. As he saw Mom laid in the decorated wooden casket, he opened the floodgates of his emotional reservoir. He immediately embraced Dad very close. Both shuddered with sobs and cries at the great loss. Judith came near the door and joined Dad and Sanjay in their embrace and cried her heart out for darling Mom. Then Sanjay went towards Maria and kissed on her forehead and started to howl very bitterly. Seeing him, everyone present there also cried for Maria. The whole neighbourhood mourned for Maria.

It was 4 O'clock and funeral band arrived. The band played hymns such as 'Nearer, my God, to Thee',

'Amazing Grace', 'Whispering Hope', 'You Raise Me Up' and the likes. The slow and heavenly music created holy and sorrowful ambience. It lifted everyone's hearts heavenwards where Maria's Soul had travelled as per the Catholic Faith.

The Priest came in, preceded by Cross and candle bearers. All of a sudden there was a pin-drop-silence. The Priest said prescribed prayers and sprinkled Holy Water on the coffin and the faithful surrounding it.

Taking that signal, the band started to play "Nearer, my God, to Thee/ There let the way appear, steps unto Heav'n /All that Thou sendest me, in mercy giv'n/Angels to beckon me nearer, my God, to Thee.'

Behind the band people started walking in a procession towards the Church. The casket was placed in the Hurst... and the last journey of Maria began towards the Church.

Vijay being well known in Social and Religious circles, thousands of people attended the funeral of his dearly beloved wife, Maria. Many Priests con-celebrated at the funeral Mass. This phenomenon had lately been acknowledged in Vasai and welcomed by the elite. It was construed that the more priests you had for the funeral meant that the dead person was holier or he/she would perhaps have an easy access to heaven. But in fact people knew that the family must be having close relations with the sacerdotal class. More than that, the concerned family's status bar went higher in the Parish TPR.

The last Rites over, once again ambience in the cemetery became holy and heavenly with the music of 'Amazing Grace' and 'Nearer, my God, to Thee' as the casket was being lowered into the grave.

After that, the immediate family members and close relatives such as brothers, sisters, uncles and aunts stood in file in order to accept condolences. That consumed more than an hour.

"Nilufer and Jasmine witnessed the whole funeral ceremony through IMO which Gabby had arranged through one of his friends.

On the funeral day Jasmine SMS'ed Vijay.

'Vijay, that was a grand funeral accorded to darling Maria.' J

'So many people attended it.' V

'Yeah…it looked like a state funeral of some political figure. Maria was looking very pretty in that dress.' J

'It's an East Indian ethnic sari…worn on the second day of the wedding, on some special occasions and lastly for the funeral.' V

'And so many ornaments! Were they real? Did they remove them all before closing the casket? I didn't see that part because too many people had crowded around.' J

'Of course, that is pure gold! They will be shared between Sanjay and Judy, as and when…' V

'The band played well, felt very heavenly and uplifted!' J

'After seventh day Mass and three days thereafter Sanjay will fly back to Melbourne. Let me know if you need anything from here.' V

'I don't need any THING…Vijay, thanks for asking.' J

The following week people kept on visiting the D'Souza's for condolence.

XXXI

Post funeral, every day was a new day for the D'Souza's,–unplanned and unexpected. Maria's loss was already a punishment for Vijay, yet to sit the whole day waiting for friends and relatives coming for condolence visits, was a bigger one. The same things were being repeated: how was your stay in Melbourne? What happened there? What was the cost of treatment there? Which doctor treated her in Mumbai? Such questions and many more had become stereotype.

Little by little Vijay started to act weird. He would look up at the ceiling and become absent to the reality around him. When a call came up for a meal, he would say he already had his food. Sanjay, Nicky and Judith concluded that Mom's death had taken his toll. They even planned to show him to a Psychiatrist.

One day as he sat in the veranda looking blank his mobile blinked with a message. Vijay had warned Jasmine never to make an IMO call.

'Hi Vijay, what's happening?'

'Nothing, just sitting idle. Tomorrow is the Seventh Day Mass. After the Mass people will come home to say prayers for the departed soul and will leave after some snacks. But close relatives and friends will come back for lunch.'

'What celebrations can these be when a very close person in the family is dead'?

'These are not celebrations but community gatherings, like an Agape. They are necessary to bring bereaved family members' routine life back to normal. The chit-chat and the gossip about social and political topics also play their role in bringing the person to normalcy in the mainstream. With people around for company the mourner starts to have regular meals. If left alone, the loneliness would harm the person mentally'. V

'Oh I see...so this tradition has a purpose?' J

'You see, the Indians are very emotional people'. V

'And what do you think we Australians are stone-hearted people?' J

'Oh no, not that way Jasmine, don't take me wrong. You see, we have a strong community bonding. In a Taluq of 15 Lakh multi-religious citizens, a 130 thousand Catholics live in closely knit villages, which have common background, common language and common social life. Therefore, we need to behave respectfully towards the elders and relatives of the community. On the other hand, suppose there are two hundred houses in a Council in Melbourne, how many families in the neighbourhood are familiar to each other? And even if they are related, are they intimate enough to share each others' sorrows and happiness?' V

'Oh, ok…I get what you mean,' J

'Vijay, do you remember I had given you an envelope at the airport, when you left from here?' J

'Oh yeah…I almost forgot about it during Maria's illness. It's in the same pocket of the jacket. I will open it today.' V

'Hope you will not be mad at me,' J

'Even if I do, you are so far away,' V

'Ok then, please don't misunderstand me,' J

'Yeah, let me read it first, then I'll get back to you tomorrow,' V

After everyone went to bed, Vijay opened the cupboard and took out the letter, opened it and reclined in bed to read it.

*****

"My dear Vijay or Mr. D'Souza,

I write this letter with immense sadness to let you know my closeness with you and your family during the bereavement of your beloved wife Maria. Maria's passing away has certainly created a vacuum first in your heart and life, then all your family members, the home and life's routine. As time passes things will get to normal, for all have to carry on with their life, until each one's turn arrives.

I am writing this letter anticipating Maria's demise. The spread was irrevocable. Oncologists Doctors discharged her for a month of Palliative care. I could not have revealed the likelihood that your Maria was in danger zone which would terminate her sooner than anyone expected. Had it happened here, it would create a horrible dent on your heart and of those in the family.

Additionally, the clearance procedures from the Hospital Authorities, the Health Ministry, the Police and the Internal Ministry, the Customs and the Airlines, to airlift the corpse to India would take almost a month to process and that would cost tremendous emotional vacuum, a desolate period, besides having to pay huge amount of money. So, I thought in my prudence that it was better for Maria to go half dead on a wheelchair than a dead body, with having to go through above rigmarole.

Vijay dear, on a personal note, any Indian including you, meeting me for the first time, will judge me promiscuous or a flirt. But that is my Sensuality Test for Men. Remember the first time I met you at the Park and I told you a lie about children being mine? That was to make you feel safe that I was married and having children and that I was a serious housewife. It was I who readily gave you my mobile number and asked you to call me. You did not call. That was a plus for you. Several times I requested you to bring Maria –*Bhabhi*- for a visit to my place but you ignored. Which meant you maintained your sobriety and self-respect.

Remember our second meeting at my place when we danced intimately? I physically applied my female trappings and you did not respond, whether because of your morality or guilt feelings, I don't know. But at that time you passed my test. Thereafter, I felt comfortable `with you anytime, anywhere.

Once you come to know the basic principles of a person, the social mores are simply put-ons to show people how holier-than-thou you are, how sanctimonious, how religious or how moral and self-righteous you are in the society.

Look Vijay, Love and Marriage are a complicated affair. Physical copulation of a male and a female is very natural and universal urge in order to procreate progeny. No sage has been exempted from it. That urge has been camouflaged or decorated by our peers with words such as love, affection, care, understanding, adjustment, reciprocity, etc. But when you love a person, sex should be the last thing that should enter one's mind. Love should be caring without any expectations, because as a social human being man's nature is to share–share emotions, share love, share bodies and also things with the loved one.

I did not get that opportunity for sharing. Not love but social custom was imposed on me; mine was just submission; just compliance to satisfy someone's beastly lust. As a child my parents and neighbours loved and cared for me immensely. But as an adult I have been physically abused and starved for real love.

I do not know why, but whenever I met you I was always filled with wonder. You sparked that glow of hope for me when I saw through you almost six months back. Your Platonic Love and my Sensuality Test would go hand-in-hand and nothing would happen! But now things for you will have changed. I know, without Maria it will be very difficult for you to pass each hour of the day. I don't know if I could fill the vacuum, but only time will tell.

Miles apart physically though, I am always in you in spirit and you in me, I suppose!

Jasmine Jennifer Singh

*****

Vijay was flabbergasted as he read that Jasmine knew from the start that Maria's illness was terminal. And she was smart enough to get them out of Australia before the Church bells tolled for Maria.

Jasmine's last phrase 'I don't know if I could fill the vacuum', provoked Vijay's mind thinking vigorously about his future. He knew however that it was too early to think on those lines at this time.

As the drowse overcast Vijay, he shoved the letter under the pillow and surrendered to oblivion.

The next day morning while doing Dada's bed Judith found Jasmine's letter. Seeing Jasmine's name below, she became inquisitive and read out the whole letter. She was astounded with the contents and called in Sanjay to read the same. Sanjay too was shocked. Both looked at each other dumfounded for a while!

The effect of the letter was very much noticeable on Vijay. He sat on the couch and hardly talked to anyone. At the same time Sanjay and Judith had to pretend they knew nothing about the letter. But after Sanjay's departure in two days' time, Vijay would be alone in the house. They had to remedy the situation. Finally they decided to talk to Dad like they had done in the garden of St. Peter's Church in Clayton.

"Judy, please keep the letter under the pillow as it was. We will talk to Dad after tomorrow's Seventh Day Mass," Sanjay suggested.

The next day morning the D'Souza family dressed in blacks for the Mass offered for the Soul of Maria. Hundreds of people came for this Mass and offered condolences to the D'Souza family in the Church compound. Close relatives and friends came home for Luncheon at which alcohol was liberally served and sumptuous East Indian dishes were prepared for the guests.

Vijay, Sanjay and Judith were formally requested and coaxed to have their fill before the guests did, in order to break the mourning barrier and start living a normal life thenceforth.

Such celebrations signify departed Soul's entry into Heaven–the Kingdom of God! As per tradition the ceremony halves anguish and helps mourners bring regularity in daily routine life. But agnostics take it as a disguise to conceal the inevitable fact of human mortality.

By early evening most of the guests had bid good-bye to the mourning D'Souza's with hugs and kisses. Only Nicky, Judith and baby Olivia remained for dinner, for they had decided to talk to Dad on that delicate issue of Jasmine's letter.

Judith left Olivia with the neighbours and upon return asked Dad sitting in the veranda that Sanjay and she wanted to have a word with him.

"Oh, yeah sure. What's the matter, dear?" said Vijay as he stood up to go to the living room.

After three of them sat on the Sofa Judith said, "Dada, Mamma left us unexpectedly and orphaned us! It is hard to accept the fact that she is no more with us, that we are never ever going to meet her again. It is difficult to ignore her presence in the house, the ambience is void of her Spirit, we miss her across each step we take in the house. We just can't imagine what you must be going through Dad, that your other half has suddenly been snatched away from your life."

"Yeah Dad, with me travelling to Melbourne the day after tomorrow and Judy being busy with her own household chores and the job, you will be left alone in the house by yourself. We are worried how you will cope with this new situation," said Sanjay with filial concern.

"Dada, besides Mumma's loss, is anything bothering you? We see you secluded and carrying on a virtual burden on your shoulders. Tell us Dada before Sanjay leaves, we can take care of the issue."

"No, nothing dear, thanks for asking though. I think I'll be able to hold myself," said Vijay resolutely.

"Do you have any external support Dad?" Sanjay asked.

"What do you mean by external support?" Vijay asked Sanjay looking directly into his eyes.

"He means that letter from Jasmine under the pillow!" Judith exploded.

"So, what about it?...She has written it, not me. Ask her if you like," said Vijay.

"You are the other party Dad, you can't disown what's written in there," said Sanjay accusingly.

"If you have read the letter without my permission that is utter violation of human rights," said Vijay vehemently.

"Did you care about Mom's human rights when you met Jasmine without her knowledge?" asked Sanjay.

"Those circumstances were typical to that situation then, you cannot generalise. Have you forgotten what I said in the garden of St. Peter's? Did you expect me to tell the lady that Mom was narrow-minded and would object to my helping her? Had I done that, as per their culture she would have lost total respect for Mom. She would not have helped us in Mom's illness the way she did. She won everyone's heart by caring for Mom. She became just like one of our family members," said Vijay with equal forte.

"That was in Melbourne Daddy. Now we are in Vasai and we have to live as per traditions prevalent here. From her letter it is very clear that she wants to establish relationship with you," said Judith.

"That's her freedom to think and act as she likes, Judy. Have I called her here to Vasai? Not even eight days have passed for my wife to have departed and do you think I am dreaming of establishing relationships, Judy? Judy, I am grieving for my loss, I am left alone and you are firing these absurd questions at me?" said Vijay and started to sob uncontrollably.

Sanjay signalled Judith with his eyes to leave Dad alone and let him release emotions by crying it out.

XXXII

The next day morning after breakfast, Sanjay, Judith and Nicky went upstairs in Sanjay's room. They called Nilufer in Melbourne on video conference call:

"Nilu darling, can you hear us clearly? I have Nicky and Judy with me in our room on the conference call," said Sanjay.

"Yeah, you are clear and loud. We are missing you darling, just one more day to go…" said Nilufer.

"Is Jasmine around?" Sanjay.

"No darling, she has gone to Coles to fetch some grocery for us."

"Oh, that's good. How's baby doing?"

"Fantastic…Jasmine is really taking great care of Ajay. I had misjudged her initially but now realize it is in their culture to behave the way she does," said Nilufer appreciating Jasmine.

"The situation is little different, Nilu," said Sanjay and continued, "Jasmine knew right from the beginning the serious nature of Mom's illness. She had known from the doctors that Mom was a guest for a couple of months. And therefore she made it possible for Mom and Dad to leave from there before occurrence of the obvious, which otherwise would have been extremely troublesome for us all," said Sanjay.

"Yeah, great...we must appreciate what she has done for us and still doing, darling."

"But it was with a tag...Nilu!" said Judith and continued, "She had written Dad a letter which was to be opened after a month and half. That is after Mom could possibly have died," said Judith with a suspenseful intonation.

"Oh yeahhh? But how did you come to know about it?" asked Nilufer.

"One morning while I was doing Dad's bed, I found the letter under his pillow. It was wrong for me to read it, but as I saw Jasmine's name beneath, I got tempted. You know what she wrote at the end?"

"No...what was it?"

"She dared to write Dad,–'But now things for you have changed. I know, without Maria it will be very difficult for you to pass each hour of the day. I don't know if I could fill the vacuum, but only time will tell.' So Nilu, we feel she has been eyeing Dad for quite some time. And with Mom gotten ill things have turned very well in her favour," said Judith condescendingly.

"Umh...Judy...I would differ from your opinion. I am going through that experience right now which Jasmine might have gone and perhaps is still going through. It is just ten days that Sanjay is away but each day is hell for me. Without him each moment of the day haunts me. I miss him every minute. Right now Jasmine is filling in for Sanjay, only materially though. I am on my job. She drops Ajay at the crèche and me to the office; and does the reverse in the evening. Without her for my company and household chores I would have gone mad," said Nilufer sympathetically.

"You mean she can be with Daddy permanently?" intervened Nicky.

"Please do not misconstrue me, Nicky. That is not for us to decide and I strongly feel that we must leave it to them to decide mutually. It's their life. We have ours with our husbands and babies. So, let them have a chance to communicate. If we put impediments at the start they won't have an opportunity to interact," said Nilufer seriously.

Seeing that conference was taking longer than expected, Sanjay came in and said, "Ok, Nilu...we heard you. Thanks for the contribution, for we got to see the other side of the mountain. I'll be there soon...with lots of kisses and hugs to you and to baby Ajay", and he put the phone off.

The three of them in the room started to stare at each other without a word for several minutes.

"Now I begin to see there is a valid point in what Nilu says. But I wonder what would be the age difference between the two of them," said Judith.

"Dad is fifty and she must be about thirty, clear twenty years apart! But she looks much younger for her age," said Sanjay.

"So does our Dad look younger for his age of fifty!" said Judith and continued, "Age does not matter at midlife point. It is the match of character and mental and emotional compatibility that is most important."

"Both stand as eligible candidates but the time is not ripe yet, Judy," said Sanjay.

"Yes brother…at least a month's mind Mass should be over before we can talk about this to Dada," said Judith.

Finally they arrived at a consensus that they would stop further discussion on this topic until Month's Mind Mass for the departed Soul of Maria was over.

Vijay, seated on an easy chair in the veranda, was reading newspapers. His mobile blinked.

'Hi, Good Afternoon!'

'It's morning here'.

'Oh, sorry…Good Morning Vijay'.

'What's so good about morning?'

'Is anything wrong dear?'

'Everything…'

'What happened?...Speak out Vijay, are you not well?'

'Your letter screwed up everything. Judy found it under my pillow and they all read it'.

'They are not supposed to read my personal letter to you, Vijay'.

'That's the drawback in our culture, however educated we Indians are!'

'Anyways, what's wrong with my letter?'

'What's wrong?? First of all you knew severity of Maria's illness. Secondly, you kept it a secret from all of us, including me. Thirdly, you wonder if you can fill the vacuum!'

'I was just being straight forward, Vijay'.

'Don't you think you encroached into this delicate emotional matter rather hastily? Weren't you romantically a bit aggressive? In this sorrowful atmosphere, you were out of tune, Jasmine, let me tell you this'.

'Yeah, come to think of it, I was! That was quite outrageous on my part. But I still say that it was between you and me, not a public document!'

'Well, the three of them went upstairs to talk to Nilufer. I do not know what happened after that. Sanjay has left here by early morning flight, he should be there soon'.

'Ok Vijay…don't you worry. I'll handle it at this end'.

Jasmine was a combination of two cultures – half Indian blood fully nurtured in Australian culture.

XXXIII

As usual Charles had brought Nilufer early morning to the airport to receive Sanjay. Baby AJ was with Nanny Jasmine. Sanjay had travelled light. He did not have any unaccompanied baggage, so he came out quickly after the flight landed.

"Hi Charlie, hi Nilu, Good Morning!" Sanjay held Nilu close to his chest and kissed her on lips. "Why didn't you bring Ajay along?"

"He is fast asleep under Nanny's care," said Nilufer.

Charles also gave Sanjay a condolence hug.

As Charles' car slowed at 504 Fulton Street, Sanjay saw Jasmine holding baby Ajay in the veranda, ready to welcome Sanjay.

"I'm very sorry Sanjay about Mom's loss. I share in your sorrow," said Jasmine as she hugged Sanjay and handed Ajay to him.

Seated in the living room Jasmine said, "Sanjay, as soon as you left, Ajay was crying after you."

"Good that you were here Jasmine, or else things would have been difficult for Nilu to manage by herself," said Sanjay in appreciation.

"I have gone through such kind of bereavement myself recently, Sanjay. I know how to face life as it comes. From our childhood we have been taught to take on any challenge," said Jasmine confidently.

"Yeah Sanjay, Jasmine told me her life-story. She has gone through hell and came out a winner," said Nilufer in support of Jasmine.

In the meantime Jasmine went to the guest room and came out with her handbag. She said, "Bye sweetheart AJ. I'll be missing you sweetie-pie."

"Where are you going Jasmine," asked Sanjay.

"Home, of course…now that you have come, I have my own things to take care of."

"Hang on till evening Jasmine, we'll have lunch together," requested Nilufer. "You know for sure Ajay won't sleep without your lullaby."

"Ok, let's hear some news from Bombay then," said Jasmine.

"Well, it was a shock for all of us, Jasmine. Only you knew Mama's beginning of the end. And you used your prudence well or else it would have been a mess," said Sanjay admirably.

"Mess…? It would have been a total chaos! Maria's body would have remained in the morgue for almost a month, with all the internal organs removed," said Jasmine with a concern.

"Jasmine, the farewell and thanksgiving party we hosted for Mom and Dad the day before they left from here, was nothing compared to the work you have done behind the curtain without letting us know about it," appreciated Sanjay and continued, "but there was also some happening which we came to know about in Vasai. First of all I must apologize on behalf of Judy that she accidently saw and read your personal letter to Dad. But knowing you well now and Dad's current situation, it is best left to you two to decide your future together. We suggest you take your time till the Month's Mind Mass is over."

Jasmine had no words to express her gratitude to Sanjay and Nilufer for their consideration. She stood up and said, "Sanjay and Nilufer I promise you and your sister Judith and Nicky that I will do whatever…wherever to keep your father happy throughout his life. This is going to be like my dream come true."

The three of them hugged and shed tears of sorrow and joy simultaneously. After lunch Jasmine rushed to her house because she had to get on the WhatsApp or IMO with Vijay. She was fired with desire to see her Vijay face to face on IMO after many days.

As soon as Jasmine left, Nilufer said, "Sanju, Jasmine is very sweet and courageous. You see, she fearlessly wrote a letter to Dad about her intention. Not even a month and if people come to know in Vasai, they will spit on Dad."

"For the Australians healing time is very short. They love easily and they forget easily too. It's their culture Nilu and they don't find anything embarrassing about it. They see their immediate happiness as life passes on," said Sanjay and continued, “You know that most famous American Hollywood star Elizabeth Taylor? She married and divorced seven husbands and one of them twice – Richard Burton!”

As Jasmine drove the car into the garage, WIFI signal sounded and she initiated WhatsApp chat with Vijay. It was morning time in Vasai.

‘Hi Vijay dear, Sanjay landed safe and sound’.

‘He called me already’.

‘Yeah, they thanked me for helping out’.

‘What else?’

‘They’re worried about your loneliness, dear’.

‘I’m not’.

‘Why should you, when I am there for you?’

‘You are there and I am here, how can you help me?’

‘So, after Month’s Mind Mass you can come here’.

‘How can I?...leaving the whole household here?’

‘Vijay, you can’t bring the household here, give its charge to Judy and Nicky and you alone come here, ok?’

‘I must ask Sanjay about it’.

‘He and Nilu have suggested so’.

‘Is that right? Ok, then I’ll start preparing’.

‘Other than that, how are you darling?’

‘Some relatives are stepping in, we’ll chat later’.

‘Ok, ciao…’

Jasmine was extremely cheerful about the events that were unfolding in her favour and as she had dreamt. That evening she rushed to the MannaCare Old-Age Home to break the good news to her Mom Jessica.

“Hi Jessica Smith Himmat Singh, how are you today?” said Jasmine as she greeted and hugged her mother.

“You have come after a long time. What held you up?” asked Jessica.

“Nothing, except that I have fallen in love.”

“You’re already late, darling?”

“It’s better late than never. It’s for the first time I have fallen in love, Mom.”

“Who’s the guy?” asked Jessica.

“Remember a month back a gentleman, Vijay by name, came with me to see you?”

“Yeah, I do. How can I forget? I saw you happiest for the first time.”

“He is a gem of a person, Mamma!”

“I am happy for you darling Jenny ... if you are happy…I am always happy,” said Jessica with halts.

There was a sudden sparkle on Jessica’s face.

“I see you very fresh and fit today, Mom. You should be ready to come home within next 15 days or so,” said Jasmine optimistically.

“*Inshallah*!” (Allah-willing) said Jessica as she had learnt some Arabic phrases on her Gulf flights.

Jasmine laughed away Mom’s wit and left the Home.

As soon as Jasmine reached home, she SMS’ed Vijay:

‘Visited Mom this evening. She’s very happy’.

‘Happy for?’

'...that I'm happy'.

'What are you happy about?'

'That my Mom is happy about you and me'.

'Take it easy dear...I am mourning here'.

'Oh, yeah...sorry darling'.

'I'm waiting for the day you will land here. I'll hug you so tight, won't leave you till we reach home'.

At home in Vasai, Nicky and Judith visited Vijay every day in the evening. Since both of them worked, Judith had arranged Tiffin meals for him. Ten days had already passed for Sanjay to have left. He and Nilufer made IMO calls to Vijay in the evenings when both Nicky and Judith would be with him.

XXXIV

A new chapter had begun in Jasmine's life. She had gone through a cloudburst with Vijay a month ago. This time she missed her menses and became frightened but also curious. At this moment of anxiety she needed someone loving, close to her. The only person she could break the news to was Vijay. After Maria's passing away, Vijay had become forlorn in his attitude. Jasmine had noticed his dejection and had resolved to bring him back on track.

'Viju darling, I am missing you very badly. Wish you were here right now. I'm not able to sleep. Thinking of us both...how will we be able to stay without each other?'

... ... (no answer from Vijay)

'Not able to sleep...sitting on the same couch... How heavenly it was to be in your amorous embrace ...thanks for giving me so much love...please for my sake, give a message soon,' your ever-loving Jasmine.

*****

'I don't much think of God but this time I wish to thank Him for sending you in my life. But when you don't respond to my pleas, I feel you are trying to avoid me. Viju, I don't want to lose you. We will be together forever till we die,' J

*****

'Viju darling, I am having temperature and severe headache. My stomach is churning and I get throwing-up feeling but nothing is coming out. I don't know what is happening to me, darling. Please come soon, I'm missing you…' J

Jasmine got exasperated that Vijay was not answering her SMSs, whether deliberately or inadvertently. She rested for half an hour, woke up and checked her mobile but there was no response. So, she straight away pressed his mobile number. It rang but no answer. After a while she tried again and someone picked up. The voice did not sound familiar, so she said,

"Hello, hello…I want to speak to Mr. Vijay D'Souza, is he around? May I speak to him, please?"

"I'm afraid you may not; he is under sedatives and Doctor has forbidden him to use the mobile till he recovers."

"Recovers from what? What happened to him?" Jasmine.

"I am only a Nurse here and cannot divulge any information to anyone calling on phone."

"May I talk to any of his relatives there? I'm calling from Australia, Jasmine…my name is…" while saying this in an upset mood the Nurse said, "No one is here, but if someone comes I will pass on the message," subsequently Jasmine's phone got disconnected.

The previous evening Vijay had skipped his evening Tiffin meal and the next day morning he had high fever combined with hallucinations and abrupt blabbering. The neighbours called Nicky and Judith. Both of them came and since Vijay was becoming fidgety and difficult to handle, they moved him to the hospital. Doctors checked him and put him under observations with cardiac monitor and some mild sedatives to keep him tranquilized.

Judith finished her scheduled work for the morning in the office and took half day off and came to the Hospital. She straight away went to father's bedside and placed her palm on his forehead. He had slight fever but was sound asleep.

The Nurse who had attended the call from Australia informed Judith about it. Judith took the phone and swiped it open and saw that Jasmine had called. She also saw that father had several messages in the box. So she opened the box and it was a shocking Pandora's Box for her eyes difficult to believe.

Judith surmised that on one hand father was recovering from mother's loss and on the other, Jasmine was pressing him for things juvenile. He was being pulled from both ends; therefore, his psychic equilibrium had given way.

Judith had already informed Sanjay and Nilufer what had happened to Dad in the morning and about his hospitalization. But now she was stunned with the new revelation and wondered how to break the news.

"Hey Brother…water between Dad and Jasmine runs much deeper than what seems to be on the surface," said Judith on the phone to Sanjay.

"What do you mean deep, and how deep?"

"As deep as you can't imagine!"

"You mean physical?"

"I guess from her SMS's."

"Judy, why do you trample on Dad's private intellectual property?"

"No Brother, the Nurse told someone from Australia called and so I wanted to see whose call it was. And those messages popped out in front of my eyes in magnified fonts! Sanjay, I suggest you call her or go visit her. Something must be drastically wrong with her."

"Ok Sis, I'll do that," said Sanjay and immediately dialed Jasmine. He made several calls but there was no response.

"Nilu, we are in a funny situation. Dad is ill and just don't know what has happened to Jasmine," Sanjay said. "C'mon, let's go to see what's wrong with Jasmine."

Sanjay rang the door bell but there was no response. They waited at the entrance for a few minutes and baby Ajay started to cry loudly. All of a sudden the door slowly opened. Jasmine was attuned to Ajay's cry more than the door bell. She looked pale and down, with unkempt hair. As soon as she saw them she started to sob. She signaled them to sit in the living room.

"What happened to Dad? Why have they kept him on sedatives?"

"We don't know what exactly is wrong with Dad, he is undergoing some pathological tests, Jasmine," said Sanjay.

"No wonder, yesterday he was quite irate and abrupt in his messages, which is not of him otherwise," said Jasmine in quivering manner.

"How is my baby AJ? I can't hold him because I am having temperature, since morning."

"Let us go to our place Jasmine, you'll feel better in our company," said Nilufer.

"No thank you Nilu, so nice of you, dear. I am on Panadol and I should be up by tomorrow," said Jasmine politely.

"Jasmine, I think if Dad is not disturbed for the next ten days, he should be on his feet by Mom's Month's Mind Mass. Doctor has told him not to use mobile phone for a week. Judy has put it off," said Sanjay politely to avoid any embarrassment.

"Can I go to India and take care of Dad, Sanjay?" said Jasmine pleadingly with her hands joined and started crying bitterly.

Sanjay and Nilufer looked at each other. They didn't know what to say.

"Umh…Jasmine you please take rest now. Shall I bring some soup for you, or some rice and Dal?" Nilufer asked.

"No Nilu thanks…I don't have taste in my mouth. I will manage with some fruits and milk; you are so caring, Nilu."

Seeing Jasmine's pathetic condition Sanjay said, "Jasmine, we are planning to get Dad here for some time. He should be here in a couple of days after the Mass."

That was unanticipated good news Sanjay had given Jasmine. So, she looked up and attempted to smile gleefully, but it was a cheerless smile after all!

Sanjay had a tough job of maintaining a balance between two cultures without hurting any party. His philosophy was: 'Since we are the recipients of a PR (Permanent Residence) from the host country, the migrants must respect sentiments of the original citizens. Certain home-country habits of talking loudly or singing Hindi/Punjabi songs in Metro or sub-way trains, showing off electric gadgets in public to tease locals, disturbs the peaceful ambience. Australians and especially the younger generation are bound to get irritated with such public exhibition. Then there are clashes and consequently fights and murders'.

The next day morning Jasmine goes to round-the-corner medical store and gets Pregnancy Test Strips. After checking she finds results are positive. Being a Nurse herself she wanted to reconfirm, so she goes in for urine test and that too comes positive.

A couple of days' stay in the hospital and Vijay was on his feet again. One day he asked, "Judy, where is my mobile phone?"

"Dad, while you were in the hospital, it fell down. It's in the repair shop. It should be ready by now. I will fetch it this evening," said Judith.

In the meantime she called Sanjay and asked if the mobile could be handed over to Dad.

"C'mon Judy, have a heart. He is our father. We can't treat him like a child. Let him have his freedom," said Sanjay.

Sanjay further said, "Judy, Dad will be only fifty this year. Let him be in a relationship if he wants to be. Suppressing sexual urges can boomerang into more complicated psychic problems. He is coming here anyway and how can we stop them from seeing each other? On the contrary if both are happy in each others' company, why not? Let them be!"

After a few days, finally that long-awaited Month's Mind Mass for the departed Soul of Maria took place in Vasai with good number of relatives and friends attending and joining in for five-course meal. The tradition dictates that as long as the guests are satisfied, the departed soul is also satisfied. It also ensures that bad omen of discontented soul on the family is averted.

Among Hindu brethren in India on 11th or 13th day of the death of a person, guests are invited for a meal. But they can partake of the meal only when a crow (Magpie) eats the food served on banana leaf out in the open. The guests wait until the crow –deemed departed person- starts to eat the food.

In keeping with what Sanjay had told Jasmine about getting Dad to Melbourne, she called Vijay on the Mass day for the first time after a week. She paid due respects to Maria and condoled Vijay:

"Life and death is not in our hands, Vijay. A month back it was Maria's turn and eventually it will be everyone else's."

"Thanks Jasmine, but don't ever think that I myself have not been missing you either," said Vijay in desperation.

"Heard from Sanjay...you will be with us soon in Melbourne. I am eagerly waiting for you, I have a great news for you darling. Viju dear, please understand me, I am alone here and the more I miss you indicates that more I love you; the more I get upset with you, means the more I want you for myself. If you do not understand this, don't worry. Come here into my arms and relax, you will find peace in here with me."

Vijay had got used to flying by now. So, this time going to Melbourne via Singapore was not as much explorative as the first time. However, since he had a two hours' halt at Changi Airport, he picked up some chocolates for baby Ajay and also some fancy ones for Jasmine.

As usual Sanjay and Charles were at the airport to receive Vijay. As he came out of the baggage section, Sanjay hugged Dad and took charge of the luggage trolley.

Suddenly there appeared Jasmine. She almost ran and clung to Vijay in an embrace. She kissed him lightly on lips to the embarrassment of Sanjay and Charles.

"How are you my darling Vijay? I'm happy to see you back in Melbourne."

As they reached the cars in the parking lot, Jasmine said, "I will take Vijay with me. You two get along with his luggage."

As soon as Jasmine came on the main road, Vijay asked, "How did you come to know my flight details, Jasmine?"

"Very simple, I asked Sanjay. Why? Did you instruct Sanjay not to divulge the info to me?"

"No Jasmine, don't get me wrong. I am asking because I did not expect you to come to the airport so early morning. Anyways, it was a pleasant surprise to see you."

"Exactly...I wanted to give you a surprise."

"Jasmine, Maria gave me the biggest surprise of my life, the mother of all surprises! This one surpasses all others surprises. Hardly 27 years of cohabitation! Henceforth I don't know how long I have to live this solitary life..." said Vijay with melancholy tone.

'*Not very long*' said Jasmine in her mind. But she did not want to intrude any further at his unstable period. So, she kept quiet thinking, time was the healer. Yet she determined to eventually get him on with normal life routine.

The entourage arrived at 504, Fulton Street. As soon as the bags were brought in the living room, Charles helped to open them. He was more interested in the parcels that came from Vasai to various families in Melbourne, including himself. Some would send East Indian Curry powder or Vindaloo masala, laddoos, sweets and also roasted grams – a very famous munching item during booze sessions. Charles collected all the parcels and rushed out as he had to attend his duty.

After having coffee and croissants Vijay held Ajay close to him and pretended to converse with the baby in a loving and playful manner.

After finishing Coffee Jasmine stood up and said, "Ok fellas, let Vijay rest and make-up for his lost sleep. If you feel fresh in the evening do drop by my place. I need some suggestions on alterations to my house." And she left.

Sanjay and Nilufer sorted various parcels that Judith and Nicky had sent with Dad.

"Oh, this is a lovely fancy box of chocolates, Dad," said Judith.

"I just picked it up from the Duty Free at Changi."

"Is it for any special person?" said Nilufer teasing Dad as she winked at Sanjay.

"Not particularly, it's for us. But if you want me to give it to Jasmine, there is another box for you."

"C'mon Nilu, let Dad take rest now, I'll get ready to go to office," said Sanjay and went to his room. Vijay went to his room and Nilufer followed Sanjay with the baby.

"Nilu, I think we should let Dad and Jasmine interact freely between them. It will be in their best interests as well as ours. Mentally they will function better and keep themselves physically fit in each others' company."

"Yeah Sanju, as it is Jasmine is already a semi-member of our family. We are all used to her, so she is not going to be an intruder anymore."

Nilufer always derived extra pleasure in teasing father-in-law whenever she got a chance, because he himself was a witty character and she liked to keep jovial atmosphere in the house. At early evening tea she said, "Dad, I didn't know besides being a Counselor you were also a Consultant Architect!"

"Why do you say so?"

"You seem to have become forgetful! Didn't Jasmine ask for your consultancy services this evening for renovation to her house?"

"Oh, yeah…thanks for reminding me dear."

"Please don't forget to take the Chocolates purchased for her, Dad." At that instant, both smiled at each other.

As usual Jasmine had kept the door slightly ajar, expecting Vijay any moment. She got inkling, perhaps by his scent, as Vijay entered through the gates. She stood up and opened the door wide and spread her arms to welcome Vijay.

The next moment she grabbed him by his shirt, pulled him inside and attacked him with her '*Amor*'! (love, romance)

She gave him a very long French kiss, and then kissed him on his cheeks, on his nose, eyes, ears and neck too.

"Couldn't you have waited for this moment to welcome me, Jasmine? The way you did it at the Airport was very awkward for me with Sanjay and Charles watching us, in a public place."

"I have noticed you Indians are very secretive about simple facts of life. It's natural Vijay and why should we worry about others?"

She felt uncomfortable standing and pulled him on the couch. Sitting next to him compactly with both her hands over his shoulders and crossing her left leg over his knees, she said, "Vijay, I will not ask you whether or not you missed me, because you were in horrible situation ever since you left from here with Maria. But I missed you every minute and each moment."

Looking into her beautiful blue eyes from very close, Vijay said to her warmly, "Jasmine, why do you love me so much? You look more beautiful than before! What's the secret?"

"What you mean what's the secret, didn't you read my messages when you were in the hospital?"

"No, I never got my mobile till after about a week. When I asked, Judy said it had fallen down and was in the repair shop."

"That means she might have read my messages and you are ignorant about them!"

"What was the secret, Jasmine?"

"It's a big, big, big news for us Vijay! Viju darling, I have missed my menses this time."

"What do you mean?"

"That means your gift has fructified in me, Vijay darling! A tiny little Viju has started to grow in my womb, Vijay Papa!" said Jasmine with laughter and pinching his nose.

"Wha.a.a.t?? How and when did it happen, Jasmine? Are you kidding me? It's impossible with me, I can't stoop so low."

"When…? You forgot your last day in Melbourne, on this very couch? You were screaming in pleasurable pain, you were in ecstasy, seventh heaven and at the end of the climax you were so drained out that you slept on this very couch like a log–a dead person!"

She got up furiously, picked her mobile from the coffee table and brought on screen his picture laying flat on the couch with his bottoms up. "See, look at this…is this you or someone else? Tell me who this is?" yelled Jasmine frantically.

"Jasmine, I don't remember a thing. Perhaps I was in a delirium. I must have been drugged or hypnotized."

"What are you talking Vijay? You may be a Counselor but I have an intuition of a woman. You were thirsty for love; you were thirsty for sex, because you did not get that from your wedded wife. I knew what was happening between the two of you. So I enticed you, for I too was famishing for sex for years together!"

"Are you sure what you are saying is true?"

"Do you want me to prove it with DNA test?"

"No, no…I mean was it really me?"

"Vija.a.ay…are you accusing me of sleeping with someone else and pushing it on you? Holding you responsible for it? I have been trying to adjust and integrate my Australian culture with your Indian way of living and how dare you doubt my integrity?"

Jasmine gasped for breath and said, "Listen, I don't need to have anything to do with a bugger like you. I saw you lonesome; I felt concern for you and said to myself, why should we waste our fleeting life without love and affection from our dear ones? If you are happy with me and I with you, why can't we make each other happy by living together? And now you doubt: 'WAS IT ME'?"

Again she huffed and said, "Get out…get out Vijay from my sight. Don't ever see my face again."

… … no one spoke for a while… …

"No, no…Jasmine, I didn't mean to hurt you, dear…"

"Don't dear me, damn it…I'm ready to do DNA test of the fetus and you will know if it was really you?"

"Sorry Jasmine, but I thought so because I had heard from an Indian that you were of a loose character."

"Who was that foolish Indian? Bring him in front of me to verify."

Now Jasmine was enraged expecting an answer from Vijay. Whereas, Vijay was perplexed and did not know what to say.

Magpie: You got to be honest buddy. Who's Bhupinder to you anyway? Once you leave from here, perhaps you won't meet him ever. But if you don't reveal his name to the lady, you'll prove yourself a coward!

"Bhupinder!" erupted Vijay.

Hearing that name Jasmine started fuming and shouting, "Oh that Punjabi bastard? He is the one who is disgracing me in the neighbourhood, then! You know in spite of him having lovely wife and two angelic children, that bastard ran after me thinking I was an easy prey for sex. He came to my house once under pretext of some Australian Punjabi Association gathering and tried to cajole. I realized his intent and just pushed him out the door. He felt insulted and started to spoil my name, with the fear that I would ruin his."

"Such are men! If they don't get what they want from a woman they will spread all kinds of rumours that will spoil an innocent person's character for life. And you have fallen prey to his tricks. You all men are same! You all know only the pussy and not what real love is!"

Having said this, Jasmine went to her bedroom, threw herself on bed and dug her head under the pillow and cried aloud.

XXXVI

The following days were busy for the D'Souza's. Every evening a family or two from Vasai East Indian Community paid them condolence visits. Even Sanjay's Goan, Mangalorean and Hindu family friends came over to console the mourning D'Souza's.

Jasmine did not turn up at the D'Souza's the next day and the next. So Nilufer started to tease Dad, "What happened to Jasmine, did you give her a hard time Dad?"

"We had an argument and she is angry with me."

"Argument at this age and stage? That too you two without being married! Then the matter must be very serious."

"Nothing serious *beta* (child); I shall visit her today."

"Take some fruits Dad, if she is not keeping too well," suggested Nilufer.

*****

Vijay rang the bell and waited…waited and waited. But the door did not open. He called Jasmine on mobile but no answer. He got desperate and banged the door with his hands. After a while the door slowly opened. Jasmine could barely walk, so she took support of the furniture and the wall to take a step forward. As soon as Vijay saw her in that condition, he held her and slowly walked her cautiously to the dining chair.

"Why have you come here? You have hurt me enough. You don't belong here! I heard the bell the first time but did not respond because I knew it was you. My door bell has gone silent for last so many years. No one rings it except you. And no one has access to my house except you. No one could ever implant in my womb except you. And now you are asking me: 'was it really me'?"

"I am extremely sorry, Jasmine, please forgive me this one time. I just can't see you in this devastated condition. I promise, I will not hurt you anymore in future."

Handing over pathology test reports to Vijay, Jasmine said, "Take these DNA test reports of the growing foetus in my womb, and yours as well. See whether or not they match. If you are satisfied then only you are welcome to stay here, or else, get lost. I am an Australian for sure but I also have Himmat Singh's valour and boldness in me."

"But how did you get my DNA report?"

"Have you forgotten that night in the hospital you tested your blood for diabetes? At that time I had told the technician to do your DNA test as well."

Vijay focused his eyes on the floor for some time. Then suddenly he looked up and said, "Keep these papers with you, darling! There is no need of them."

"What did you say,...darling? The first time ever!" shouted Jasmine excitedly and held Vijay's hands resting on the dining table.

"Yes darling Jasmine. I took time to study you. Being already married, I couldn't have betrayed my Maria and broken my matrimonial promise to her. Now that she has left this world, I can be more comfortable with you. I faintly remember that morning; I was in the ether world. That pleasurable time simply evaporated from my rational mind. Only when you pulled the door locked, I woke up to my senses. I went to the mall and had a cup of coffee. At that time I was also more bogged down with anxiety about Maria and me travelling home."

After a brief pause Vijay continued, "Shall I tell you one thing Jasmine? "

"What??" Jasmine looked at him with a suspenseful face.

"You look more charming when you get angry with me. You are marvelous and so beautiful! You have given meaning to my remaining life. You have become a reason for me to get up in the morning and kiss my sleeping angel!"

Having heard this from Vijay, Jasmine didn't miss a moment but to land her lips on his. After a while, taking a break from smooching, Vijay pushed her a little farther from him. Softly and lovingly touching Jasmine's tummy, he said, "But how are you going to hide this bump, could we terminate it?"

"Only over my dead body, Vijay," shouted Jasmine. "That's a gift from God and you are only an instrument in His creation. I value human life and no one has any right to take it away. Just imagine, if your parents had done that to you as a foetus, would you be existing today, at this very moment with me? Would you be able to create a new progeny in God's image and yours?" Jasmine made a very strong pro-life statement.

"But then how are we going to face the society, Jasmine?"

"Don't you worry about society, Vijay. We can make it official as soon as possible, leave it to me."

Having said that Jasmine stood up, held his hand to make him get up. Leaning on his shoulder she directed him to the bedroom. She clung to him face-to-face in standing position and said, "I desire you Vijay and let us consummate…."

"But we are not married, Jasmine!"

"Well, that is just a formality; we are already married month and a half ago, when we gave our hearts and bodies to each other. And the symbol of our love that is growing in my womb is a witness to it."

The next moment both love-birds started to satiate each other. Sensual feeling is just as innocent and a part of one's body. As body grows so do feelings get more matured with age.

Thereafter, Vijay was more in cohabitation with Jasmine than at Sanjay's house. They lived together and loved each other more than perhaps if they were married.

The greatest success of a live-in relationship is to keep the suspense ever dynamic: The apprehension that any one of the party could break the contract any time and for any reason! Vijay always believed that for a successful relationship one had to forego one's Ego. Without dissolving the ego one could never maintain a relationship for a long time.

One evening Vijay and Jasmine walked down to the Princess Highway Reserve Park for a walk to revive their not-very-old-memories. They were seated on the same garden bench and all of a sudden the original Magpie hopped on the table-top. He looked up and down at both of them; took two steps further; turned and twisted his neck, made deep guttural sounds as if welcoming Vijay once again to Melbourne.

"Jasmine, we don't have this kind of Raven in India. What we have is either pitch black, dark brown or shiny blue, but never black and white."

"What do you want to imply."

"This fellow has been my friend and companion from the very moment I saw him on this very table-top on my first visit to the Park. It is difficult for me to say whether it is he or she. As she, she sort of fell in love with me at first sight! And at this very moment again she is with me. As he, he always stood by me as my voice of conscience. Before I took any decision, the Magpie always filtered my thought process and prompted me accordingly."

Jasmine spread her palm on the table and said: "Hello birdie, come…come, come sit on my palm if you represented me, I'll caress you, I'll take you home to feed."

The crow literally took steps and came near Jasmine's wrist and being true to its scavenging nature, it started to peck her palm. The long thick and powerful beak pierced through her tender skin and it started to bleed.

Magpie: This is my way of signing the friendship bond…with blood!

Vijay cautioned Jasmine not to play anymore with the Magpie and took her to the Community Centre's First Aid Box to apply antiseptic cream and stick a Bandage.

Both the love-birds strolled back to their house. To their surprise, the Magpie was sitting on the wooden railing at the entrance of her house. As he saw them, he produced a sub-song with rattles and clicks to welcome them.

As days and weeks passed, Jasmine became apprehensive about her growing bump. Therefore, to avert discomfort of a scandal and in keeping with social mores, Vijay and Jasmine decided to make it official.

One fine day while visiting the D'Souza's Jasmine said during the course of conversation, "Sanjay and Nilufer, you both know how Dad and I love each other; so much so that we cannot live for a minute without each other. Even the Magpies, the parrots, thc nightingales and the pigeons in the vicinity have got used to us as a couple. Let's not keep it a 'secret' anymore."

"Yeah...we see both of you very happy and inseparable. So, what are your plans," asked Sanjay.

"It's not just simple happiness, it's more than that, Sanjay," said Jasmine with a smile.

"What do you mean?" Nilufer asked.

"I mean...ummh...I have missed my menstruation cycle."

"Wow! Don't tell me that Jasmine ...congratulations! What a good news! But when did it happen?" asked Nilufer.

"Forget the when and the how of it, Nilu...that was *Amor*. Now let us look into the future."

"Oh, I must announce the good news to Judy that Sanjay and she are going to get a step-brother or step-sister!"

During this conversation Vijay just kept quiet and focused his eyes on the floor.

Sanjay was sort of aware of some happenings, so it was not an exciting revelation for him.

"We have planned to get officially married both civilly and in the Church too. We will fill the forms at the local Council Office. My Mom is fit to come home and I will fetch her tomorrow. On Friday we all will go to the office of the Local Council's Registrar for marriage registration. Mr. Brown, your neighbour, will stand witness on my behalf. I have already spoken to Mr. and Mrs. Brown about it and they happily accepted the responsibility." Jasmine took a deep breath and continued, "And on Sunday we have planned to bless the nuptials at a special Holy Mass."

"Wow, great...let's get on with your plans. I will announce them to Judith and Nicky; and invite Vasai Community people over the internet and via SMS messaging," said Nilufer.

"Dad, today is Tuesday and there aren't many days left for preparations. We will go to Little Collins Street where we will find many International Brands of Men's wear, such as: Godwin Charli, Givenchy, Gran Sasso, Harrolds, Saint Laurent, Carlucci, Gucci and so on," said Sanjay.

"Sanjay, we too will accompany you to select a wedding dress for Jasmine. Drop us at the street where we can visit outlets like Bluebell Bridal, Henry Roth, Anna Campbell, Bridal Boutique, Mariana Hardwick or Annette of Melbourne," Nilufer said.

"Of course we do not plan for a red-carpet event. I think we'll go for some simpler brands," said Jasmine to cut the budget short.

"Ok, dear I agree with you, but at least we'll do some market research and compare prevalent styles and their price tags," said Sanjay.

All the purchases were done, forms filled and registration completed, Video shooting and photographer engaged, parish hall booked for simple wedding reception, the caterers given contract. But when the question arose of the Best Man and the Bridesmaid, everyone started looking at one another's faces, as if caught in between bull's horns.

Suddenly Jasmine stood up and said, "I have a proposal."

Everyone started to gape at her. She said, "We don't have any bachelors and spinsters around. Vijay's best friend is Sanjay and my best friend is Nilufer. Therefore, the 'Bestman' will be Sanjay and the 'Bridesmaid' Nilufer. No questions asked and no objections raised, that's fixed." Jasmine declared.

She further continued and said, "And please allow my Mom to lead the Bride to the Altar during the entrance hymn in the Chapel."

Every one nodded heads and Sanjay said, "Oh, of course…that's her right and privilege,"

But Nilufer declined the offer, saying she was not going to be in shape during those days.

"Ok, in that case we excuse you. I'll ask one of my other friends, leave it me," said Jasmine.

Being quiet all the time Vijay broke the ice and said, "We must inform Judy and Nicky about the developments at this end."

"Leave it to me Vijay, I'll inform them about the developments here," said Jasmine.

XXXVII

Jasmine was required to give one month's written notice to the Registrar of the Marriage Bureau at Clayton Council of their intention to marry. But due to their specific circumstances she had managed to condone it to one week.

The next two days went pretty quick in preparation for the event. On Thursday Jasmine went to the MannaCare Home and fetched her Mom Jessica to her house.

On Friday morning Vijay and Jasmine, Sanjay and Nilufer, Mr. and Mrs. Brown went to the Office of the Registrar at Clayton Council for official registration of Civil Marriage.

The Honourable Registrar welcomed them in his Chamber and announced names of the Bride and the Groom to come forward. The Registrar then read out what marriage meant and made both the Bride and the Groom repeat specific phrases, giving free mutual consent to becoming husband and wife, in the name of God and in observance of Civic Laws.

Then the Registrar further made them sit and had them sign three Marriage Certificates in prescribed boxes. Likewise, Mr. Brown signed on behalf of Mrs. Jasmine Vijay D'Souza and Sanjay signed on behalf of Mr. Vijay Manuel D'Souza. And finally the Registrar himself signed the Certificates.

Instantly, the Registrar got up from his chair and said solemnly: "I declare Vijay Manuel D'Souza and Jasmine Vijay D'Souza as husband and wife. There were claps in the chamber, but only of the two witnesses and two supporters. The Registrar then shook hands and congratulated the newly married couple. At that time Jasmine spread her arms wide open, held Vijay in her embrace and kissed him, 'Happy life till death do us part'!

The Registrar then handed over one Marriage Certificate to Vijay and Jasmine for their records, the second copy he reserved for the Registry of Births, Deaths and Marriages Department and the third he kept for his office records.

The entourage rushed home for Sunday's preparations. The special wedding mass arranged with the Parish Priest of St. Peter's was at 5 pm.

Sanjay contacted decorators and told them to be at the Church hall on Sunday morning to put up decorations and caterers to be ready with preordered menu by 6 pm.

Vijay had befriended a Pakistani Muslim barber, Yousuf Khan in a Saloon at one of the Malls. Yousuf volunteered to dress, groom and style Vijay free of cost, provided he was invited to witness the Catholic wedding and reception in the hall.

Mr. Vijay D'Souza the Groom was decked up with a smart youthful hairdo, blue suite and Berluti Alessandro calf leather shoes. By 4 pm quite a few Vasaikars gathered at Sanjay's place to take the Bridegroom to the Church.

Mr. Brown went to bring the Bride. Jasmine-Jennifer Himmat Singh-Smith was dressed up by the famous Beautician in town. Her Wedding Gown sparkled with tiny American Diamonds. She wore a beautiful crown studded with precious stones. And above all she did not forget to wear the sparkling set of Swarovski bracelets, presented by the D'Souza's in memory of late Maria. As they arrived at the Church, there were already about fifty people occupying front pews in the nave of the Church and many more kept coming.

Both parties stood in file at the main door of the Church, but there was no sign of the Bridesmaid. Time was ticking…just a few minutes to 5 pm.

The Organist had started playing prelude tunes to set the faithful in a sanctified mood. All in the procession became anxious as Jasmine was frantically calling someone every minute.

"What's happening? Where is your Bridesmaid?" Vijay asked Jasmine.

"She should be here any moment now."

"Is she coming by car or chopper?"

"This is no time to joke darling. I think we have to go without her."

Taking a cue from Jasmine and in support, Vijay whispered into Sanjay's ears: "Go tell the Celebrant Priest to hold on for five minutes, we are awaiting the Bridesmaid."

Just then the bell in the sacristy sounded Priest's entry to the Altar and the Organ started to play the wedding hymn.

Sanjay managed to reach the Sacristy door and held the curtain which the Altar Boy was trying to open for Priest's entry towards the Altar.

"Please Father, could you hold on for just five minutes, the Bridesmaid should be here any moment now."

"Don't worry about her. Is she going to replace the Bride?" said the Reverend sarcastically.

With that straight-ball wicket, Sanjay didn't have any answer but to yield. Soon after, Vijay and Sanjay holding hands followed by Jasmine and Jessica and the little angelic flower-girls, in beautiful pink dresses started to take slow steps.

Many from the congregation, especially the Indian ones, giggled heartily at the scenario. For, normally the father leads the son towards the Altar of Matrimony, whereas, here it was just the opposite.

Hardly five steps in and there rushed the Bridesmaid and synchronized with Jasmine's marching steps. Jasmine looked at her left and gave a broad smile. The Bridesmaid reciprocated with a sigh and panted heavily.

As the procession advanced at a snail's pace towards the Altar, to everyone's utter surprise the long awaited Bridesmaid was none other than Judith Fernandes. Judith from Vasai appeared literally out of the blues and made just in time for the nuptials! It was certainly a pleasant surprise to everyone present.

The nuptials were blessed by Rev. Fr. Nelson Bashir, Catholic Priest from Karachi, Pakistan, posted in Clayton parish six month ago. He summoned the couple closer to the Altar along with the witnesses.

Fr. Bashir said, “Vijay and Jasmine, the promise you make to each other today is serious, because it will bind you together for life in a relationship so close and so intimate that it will profoundly influence your whole future. That future, with its hopes and disappointments, its successes and its failures, its pleasures and its pains, its joys and its sorrows, is hidden from your eyes. You know that these elements are mingled in every life and are to be expected in your own. And so, not knowing what is before you, but trusting in God’s companionship, you take each other through the best and worst of what lies ahead, until death. I now invite you to join hands, and commit yourselves to each other forever.”

Already six months in, Fr. Nelson had not yet picked up the Australian diction. His attempt to imitate Australian articulation produced funny pronunciations, difficult to decipher even simple words. The Indians started looking at each others’ faces. It was not even close to Indian English, but pure Pakie!

The Priest continued, “Vijay and Jasmine, have you come together freely and without reservation to give yourselves to each other in marriage?”

“Yes, we have,” said Vijay and Jasmine in unison.

“Will you love and honour each other as husband and wife for the rest of your lives?”

“Yes, we will.”

“Will you accept children lovingly from God and bring them up according to the law of Christ and His Church?”

Should I say yes to this or no? I am not sure what will happen to our child when he becomes an adult. How can I declare it for sure right now? Thought Jasmine, but she yielded to the question as a formality…

"Yes, we will," said Vijay and Jasmine; they smiled at each other, thinking about the child in her womb witnessing their marriage!

"Since it is your intention to enter into marriage, join your hands and declare your consent before God, your family and friends," said Fr. Bashir and handed Vijay the text.

Holding Jasmine's right hand, Vijay, the Bridegroom solemnly read: "I, Vijay, take you Jasmine, to be my lawfully wedded wife. I promise to be true to you in good times and in bad, in sickness and in health. I will love you and honour you all the days of my life."

Similarly Jasmine, the Bride said: "I, Jasmine, take you Vijay, to be my lawfully wedded husband. I promise to be true to you in good times and in bad, in sickness and in health. I will love you and honour you all the days of my life."

Thereafter the Priest said, "You have declared your consent before your families and friends and God. May the Lord strengthen your consent, and fill you both with His blessings. What God has joined together, let no one put it asunder."

Then while blessing the rings with the Holy Water the Priest said, "Lord, bless these rings which we bless in your name. Grant that those who wear them may always have deep faith in each other, may they do your will and always live together in peace, good will, and love. We ask this through Christ our Lord. Amen."

Then placing the ring on Jasmine's ring finger, Vijay said, "Jasmine, take this ring as a sign of my love and fidelity." In return, Jasmine did likewise.

At the end of the Nuptial ceremony Fr. Bashir gave a solemn blessing, "May you always bear witness to the love of God in this world so that the afflicted and the needy will find in you generous friends and welcome you into the joys of heaven. Amen."

Then he said, "Now you may kiss each other as husband and wife."

Bearing the sanctified décor of the place in mind Jasmine restrained her libido and just tapped Vijay's lips gently with hers, this time, like a bird pecking on a morsel of food.

After the sacrament of Matrimony was over, the assisting Priest signaled them to turn back.

"What a great surprise you have given us all, Judy," whispered Sanjay into her ear while the newly married couple went to the prie-dieu.

After the wedding Mass, the newly married couple and witnesses went to the Sacristy to sign the Church Registers.

Magpie: You see Vijay, finally I have won. I had warned in the very beginning to be on your guards, but you let loose. Now, forever you belong to her.

What the hell are you doing here in this holy place? Who allowed you in here Magpie? Leave me alone right now. We can talk later on....

There was a photography session of the family members, relatives and friends with the newly married couple in the Church garden.

Various groups gathered round the newly wedded couple to pose for pictures. Later as Vijay and Jasmine were directed to give various poses with different backgrounds, they were also seated on the lawn for a picture pose. Suddenly, they heard caws of the Magpie and next moment he landed from the branch above in their front. They were aghast to see their third partner with his usual grating coos and rattles. The photographer rushed to shoo the crow away but Jasmine yelled, "Let him be, let it be…he's our guest, invited for the wedding."

The Magpie tilted his head up and down indicating his approval this time. He dared to hop on Vijay's shoulder from Jasmine's side and posed for a picture, while Vijay and Jasmine sealed their threesome relationship with a prolonged kiss. No one could ever guess what was happening!

Charles approached the couple and said, "There's only an hour left for the reception to start. You still have to go to the Honeymoon Suite for changing and et cetera."

The wedding Limousine brought them to Waverley International Hotel. As they entered their Honeymoon Suite Jasmine put her arms round Vijay's shoulders and closed the door with her leg in reverse and dimmed the lights.

They soon brought into reality the significance of 'Honeymoon Suite'. Having been exhausted from sensual calisthenics, Jasmine whispered into Vijay's ears, "Honey I don't feel like getting out of your embrace. Wish I could remain in this position till I die!" said Jasmine being worked up emotionally.

"Darling, we have to dress up for the reception, c'mon, let's hurry, dress up and call the beauticians," said Vijay in excitement.

The rest of the guests walked towards the wedding hall behind the Church. Giving baby Ajay to Judith Nilufer said, “That was a fantastic surprise Judy. How did you manage all that with such a short notice?”

Nicky intervened and said, “Jasmine had already informed us about the wedding plans and to be ready to travel to Melbourne for a week. She warned us strictly not to divulge about our coming to Melbourne. She had also said that if Nilufer refused to be Bridesmaid, Judy should fill in. As requested Judy sent her gown measurements via SMS to Jasmine.”

Judy added, “The flight was delayed and we were frantically worried about reaching in time. Charles picked us up 3.30 pm from the airport and took us to his house to dress up. Thanks to God we made just in time to the Chapel!”

As the Master of Ceremony announced arrival of the Bridal entourage into the hall, the DJ started to play the Royal Wedding Reception March. About 150 guests had lined-up along the aisles with graffiti in their hands to shower on the couple.

The parading over, the cake was cut to the tune of ‘Congratulations’ by Cliff Richards; frothing Champagne opened and sprayed; pictures being clicked; Mr. Brown raising the toast; the event being enjoyed with claps galore for the newly wedded couple: Mr. Vijay Manuel D’Souza and Mrs. Jasmine Vijay D’Souza. Vijay and Jasmine being happiest couple on earth that moment, replied to the Toast and thanked all guests.

Jasmine looked incredibly gorgeous, blooming with youthful pink at thirty and Vijay, a handsome groom at fifty. It was their first wedding dance to the tune of

'You Are Beautiful' by James Blunt. They waltzed slow with impeccable steps and moves. By and by, the MC requested guests to join in with the newly-wedded couple, dancing their first official dance of married life. The floor was almost full and the scene looked spectacular. Later numbers stirred up some couples for Foxtrots, Jive, Tango and Salsa. Many Vasaikars too had an opportunity to try their western dance abilities.

Sumptuous Dinner was served, mementos gifted to parting guests, who thanked Sanjay-Nilufer and Nicky-Judith for a wonderful wedding celebration.

Jasmine pulled Vijay towards the entrance of the hall followed by spinsters, and facing the hall she blindly flung her flower bouquet over her head behind her in the crowd. She did not wait to see which of the spinsters was lucky to grab the next wedding!

Vijay and Jasmine were showered with gifts from relatives and friends. The Limo was waiting for them at the entrance of the hall, to take them to the Hotel to change and pick up their luggage and rush them to the airport for their flight to Bali.

As guests walked towards the parking lot, Emily, Grace and Josephine from Vasai group were gossiping.

Emily said, "Just over a month for Maria's demise and couldn't they have waited at least for a year to celebrate the wedding? What was the hurry?"

Grace immediately retorted, "Here people don't care about the dead like we Indians do back home. Once a person is gone no one can get him back, so what's the use of crying over spilt milk?

"No....I have heard something else, not sure though," intervened Josephine.

"What is it Josephine?" asked Emily.

"I heard she's carrying..."

"What? My goodness! Shameless people! How could they cheat on Maria aunt?" yelled Emily.

Grace silenced them saying, "Don't you worry about Indian or Aussie. Everybody does whatever, when it is brought upon him or hcr. It's nonc of our business. Jesus said, 'Do not judge anyone' and what are you doing now? Are you worried about that Scarlet, the way she is behaving and how she is spoiling the Gonsalves family name and that of Vasai Community in Melbourne?

"Hey...hey...you better cool down, let us stop it here, people are listening to us. We will discuss this issue at Josephine's place when we meet there for Kitty party," said Emily.

XXXVIII

Destination Honeymoon in Bali! Garuda Airline's Boeing 737 window seats were reserved by Jasmine. Until take off and airborne, Vijay didn't say a word. When Jasmine finished surfing through Airline's Magazine, looking at duty-free items, she elbowed him gently thinking that he was fast asleep.

He was not. Vijay opened his left eye turned it 90 degrees and upping his left eyebrow, asked Jasmine what she wanted. She understood his mime and said: "What's the matter with you? Why are you not talking to me?"

"Jasmine, I was wondering if our wedding followed by reception were dream. In Vasai we never had our wedding in that style. At that time, ours was a village type event with most of the things home-made. Moreover, it's just one and a half month for Maria to have left us. Why did we have to rush, could we have not waited for some time to settle down?"

"Did you wish that our son or daughter, whoever it may be, to be a flower-girl for her parents' wedding?"

"Not so-far-fetched, but at least six months' wait?"

"Darling, it's natural that everyone has to die one day. It's a matter of time and how. I did not wish you to waste precious time of your life grieving. We do not know how much life is left in store for each one of us. Let's be practical, Vijay."

"It's alright for Australian culture but for us Indian's this could be very shameful."

"Why worry Vijay, do not think of Vasai anymore?"

"What do you mean?"

"I mean as my husband you are officially recognized as an Australian citizen."

"So, having lost my Indian wife, have I to lose my Indian identity too?"

"Vijay darling, please don't think negatively. Look ahead of us, what a wonderful life we will have together, with our cute little baby? Didn't you pay attention to what Fr. Bashir said as he blessed our nuptials?"

Magpie, magpie where are you? Where are you hiding now? Give me counsel...

Magpie: I can't fly to the height you are at now. Thirty-five thousand feet up and I'll freeze to death. Only thing I can say you were warned at the beginning but you did not listen to me. Now, Maria does not exist anymore and I doubt you'll get an Australian like Jasmine to take care of you and your progeny. That's why I nodded a 'yes' on the lawns of St. Peter's after you got married. Now you should make the best of what is remaining of your life. Do not regret about the past now! Look ahead what's in store for you. I'll be always with you.

Not getting any response from Vijay, Jasmine continued: "Remember Vijay what that Priest said, 'the future, with its hopes and disappointments, its successes and its failures, its pleasures and its pains, its joys and its sorrows", are not evident right now.' So, not knowing what is laid before us, we need to trust in God's companionship. Let us take each other through the best and worst of what lies ahead, Vijay."

"I mean, for a second wedding like ours, did we need to follow all formalities as if we were marrying the first time, Jasmine?" said Vijay in a resigned tone.

"Vijay, this is my first honeymoon too. I did not have a marriage ceremony like this the first time." She further continued, "After all, honeymoon should not necessarily be associated with sex alone, for it gives the couple some time in solitude, to come to know each other totally, to be transparent not only psychologically but physically too, to remove that 'otherness' feeling normally associated with less known persons, two bodies and two minds to be totally one by right of the civic law and God's mandate, which no one else can share in their future life."

After listening to Jasmine's oration, Vijay had barely forty winks sleep, only to be awakened early Monday morning by a sudden loud touchdown tire screech of Boeing 737 at Bali Ngurah Rai International Airport, also known as Denpasar International Airport. Coming out of the airport terminal, Jasmine immediately spotted a man holding a placard flashing their names. Within half an hour they were at the Four Seasons Resort at Jimbaran beach.

Jimbaran is a fishing village and coastal resort south of Kuta in Bali. Jimbaran Bay has a long beach with calm waters. It's lined with fish restaurants and backed by tropical forest. At its northern end, colorful boats are pulled up at a thriving open-air fish market.

At that early hour of the matins, the couple was welcomed with tea and cookies. Soon afterwards they hit the bed, only to wake up at lunch time.

Four days' honeymoon package included water surfing, speed boating, scuba diving in the coral reefs, snorkeling and excursion into the rain forest. Vijay and Jasmine were experiencing the ultimate in romantic escapism and wedded bliss while on this trip.

Onc of the days, Vijay along with Jasmine took the helm of motorized dinghy and discovered the many pristine bays and reefs that fringe southernmost parts of Kuta. They were given a chef-prepared gourmet picnic hamper to spend hours in absolute isolation on any of the small islands that outnumbered tourists.

Alternatively, Jasmine simply shut off from the outside world and preferred a unique indigenously inspired treatment at the Spa along with Vijay.

One evening Vijay and Jasmine enjoyed a private dinner on the pier, backlit by the sun's setting rays over the Coral Sea. Their intimate dinner for two was served under a starlit canopy and minimal interruptions that ensured a unique and romantic dining experience. Soft and slow music enhanced the romantic mood. Incidentally 'the last waltz' started to play. Jasmine reminded Vijay of the very number and their first dance in her house. She immediately pulled him in her embrace, swinging away loving memories.

After Dinner both of them were dropped at an uninhabited and totally isolated small moonlit island for four hours. There was a tent with a bed inside, a fridge full of sodas, beer and coconut water. Should any untoward incident occur, they were told to press the SOS button and guards would attend to them instantly.

The dinner and dance had already warmed up the honeymoon couple for real action. This was going to be an ultimate pinnacle of honeymoon bliss, a heaven on earth, as some call it. Except that Jasmine had to be extra careful with her delicate physical condition.

Magpie: So, she finally fulfilled her dreams of having you. It will be fine as long as both of you remain faithful to each other and respect each one's unique personality.

Not here again Magpie, which flight did you fly by?

Magpie: I don't need to fly by any flight, 'cause though I have my wings, I am always within you.

The package was full of unforgettable adventures with some superb interludes.

On one such sunset evening both Vijay and Jasmine were idling on golden sands of Jimbaran.

"Doesn't this place remind you of someone, Jasmine?"

"Who exactly?"

"See the first three letters of this place?"

"Vijay, he was never in my heart or in my life and is out of my mind ever since. Why do you want to hurt me by reminding me of that scoundrel again and again?"

"Jasmine, this is just for the sake of discussion, do not take me seriously please. Tell me, what was the real cause of your break-up?"

"Let me tell you frankly Vijay. First of all he forced himself on me at the hospital and got his friends to convince my Dad Himmat Singh for marriage. Secondly, he used to maltreat me. Then I used to run to my parents and sob in my mom's embrace. Then Himmat threatened him not to step at his house, or he would lodge a police complaint and get him arrested for molesting wife."

"Yeah, but why did he do that in the first place?"

"He was an animal, Viju. Vast difference between your way of loving me and his! He treated me like a slave because he always said that I was a migrant's daughter."

"What?... ... But your mother was an Australian, wasn't she?"

"Yeah, but he conveniently ignored it, because he did not have class. He even insulted me in pubs and casinos by passing derogatory remarks about my Indian inheritance."

"How could he ever think that way? All are God's children and have a right to live and move about freely wherever they can sustain themselves and live with absolute human respect," said Vijay to sooth Jasmine.

"I mean, from the beginning of humankind people have always been moving from place to place, from country to county and from continent to continent. And it has been beneficial to both the immigrants and host countries. So, where's the problem for these freaks!?" said Jasmine pulling Vijay on her chest and facing him upwards.

"Darling Viju, I'm extremely happy to be with you till I die. Touch wood, no one should cast an 'evil eye' on us, as my Himmat Singh used to say. And that's why he used to accompany his beautiful wife wherever she went, in his original Punjabi outfit. I am sure you will take care of me as my Dad looked after my Mom. We must get going now, lest we miss our shopping."

That last evening, Vijay and Jasmine walked with locked hands and shopped in the local bazaar for handicraft souvenirs and memorabilia for friends and relatives. Packed their bags and got ready for the flight early next day morning.

XXXIX

One can thatch away billions of Dollars into Swizz banks without revealing, hide most important secrets of science or hold back the trigger of WW-III, but one cannot hide the effects of micro-organic sperm being developed into an embryo-foetus in the womb.

After 3-4 months Jasmine's bump became quite evident. Regular check-ups and visits to Gynic kept her literally in the pink of health.

In the meantime Vijay's Naturalization process for citizenship as a dependent spouse had been initiated through the lawyer.

Back in Vasai, some of D'Souza clan's inherited property was being forcibly purchased by Builder's Lobby in Vasai. As a result, Vijay had to present himself in front of the Revenue Officer and sign some documents.

"Viju, can you not delegate your powers to someone there, Nicky and Judith are already there and won't they manage," pleaded Jasmine.

"I'm not doing this deliberately darling. You think I will be comfortable there without you? Mentally I will always be here with you, you know that, Jasmine."

"I am worried Viju; I have to manage my Mummy and the baby in my tummy. I'll miss your loving touch on my abdomen and your ears listening to its movements."

"Could we work out this way then: you could keep Mom temporarily at MannaCare and you would stay with Sanjay? That way I won't have to worry about you all the time. It's a question of only ten days darling."

"Yeah, that sounds like a good idea, we could do that. I'll check with the MannaCare if they have a vacant room. But promise you will not stay a minute more once your work is done."

"Ok darling…as you wish!" said Vijay holding Jasmine intimately close to him and kissing her.

*****

From the moment Vijay landed at Schatrapati Shivaji International Airport in Mumbai (Bombay), Jasmine kept his track from time to time. When he could not converse, she sent him messages galore.

"Darling Viju, I am alone reclining in the couch thinking of you...what my Viju must be doing right now? Please give message I am missing you a lot."

"Honey, I can't describe how much I missed you ever since I've landed here. Getting used to it now…have to run up and down a lot. You don't know how corrupt the Indian bureaucracy is. Unlike in Melbourne, here we have to bribe civil servants from top to bottom. Very very frustrating!...Sheer waste of time and energy!"

"Viju, think of me and our baby...that will lighten your burden…you will have a cause for what you're doing."… "Darling, I don't know how to write…do you remember our first time?...I'll never forget that day in my life… the way I made love with you was so exhilarating! While writing all this you should understand how much I am missing you and I feel like making love with you right now."

"How heavenly it is to be in your loving embrace, Jasmine. My day will go well with your simple assurance that you are mine alone. Darling thanks for the pleasant time you give me."

"I am jealous of you Viju, I envy you, I argue and fight with you, I command you, yet I beg of you. But above all I love you from the bottom of my heart. Why?...What magic have you done to me, love?"

"Please ask yourself what hypnotism you have exercised on me."

"I have been kissing you on my mobile screen to the extent that I need to laundry it now." …"Love come close and swipe your lips gently on mine and let me feel the thrill and vibration of your intimacy. It makes me long for your loving words and tender touch."

*****

Another two days were left for Vijay to return to Melbourne. Nicky and Judith were getting a few condiments for Sanjay's kitchen and other knick-knacks.

"Hi Papa, what's happening? Time for you leave once again," said Judith while placing the suitcase on the floor.

"Yeah, just today and tomorrow…early Wednesday I will be air-borne."

"Did you sign all the documents at Registration Office, Papa?"

"Yeah Judy…thank Goodness the imbroglio is over once-and-for-all. Three generations' names were not recorded…it took a long time to update all the documents. Sale deed and conveyance was done and our one-eight share, I have divided between the three of us."

"Why Papa…now that you have your own family, you should have kept the whole amount for yourself."

"No, no…I wouldn't do that. Plus there are several other agricultural plots. Sanjay's and your names have been added to the seven-twelve extracts. I have handed over all the documents to Nicky for your ownership records."

"Papa…I was wondering if I could ask you a personal question."

"Yeah, go ahead…be open. You are my daughter…that's ok. And now that you are married, you are my friend too."

"How are you two getting along, Papa? I am sure despite 20 years age difference between you and Jasmine, you two must be doing pretty well!"

"Oh fantastic, Judy…she is very lovable, understanding, intelligent and hardworking. She takes care of me minutely, to the last detail. She likes to see me happy always. And I reciprocate too."

"Despite Mom's sudden departure, all of us feel very happy for you, Papa!"

"Judy, it could only happen in Australia, Europe or USA. But not in India, until may be after a year or two. And that's a huge cultural gap to adjust with, for Indian migrants in foreign countries."

"Moreover, we came to know Jasmine from very close and her genuine character. And felt that she was best suited for you, Papa."

"Judy, you know I have been associated with family affairs and working towards social harmony throughout my adult life. Our findings reveal that discord between husband and wife begins with differences of opinions, followed by arguments and fights."

Vijay took deep breath and continued, "Once man and a woman get married and see each other's body naked and do all sorts of callisthenics during sex, they eventually come to a realization that the mystery of love, emotions and the curiosity of seeing and fondling of genitals remains no more a mystery. Once the carnal desire is satiated repeatedly, the partners become dispassionate towards physical urge. Subsequently partners lose incessant desire for sexual relationship. At this point deep spiritual aspect of love in union with God (the other partner) plays very important role. Lack of spirituality in married life takes precedence over shallow attitude towards that union as satisfying one's natural physical craving. It disregards the spiritual role of the matrimonial union between man and woman."

Vijay continued further, "Judy, Jasmine is indeed gem-of-a-person. But generally once the newness of intimacy between married partners evaporates, especially after arrival of a child, small misunderstandings become big issues. First of all, after the delivery, woman's world changes drastically. The husband is deprived of wife's normal kind of love which is divided between him and the infant. So the husband finds it very hard to adjust to that sudden change in wife's attitude. That attitude is brought about by certain priorities of the infant over those of the husband. And that is the root cause of discord between otherwise very loving and understanding couple. Finally what matters is deep and sincere love and adjustment between the two, along with unwavering faith in each other, for betterment of the child."

"Papa, you are the Master in these affairs and we only hope that everything goes well with her delivery. We are praying for that."

"Well, I have an inkling that my Maria is going to come back…" and suddenly Vijay burst out weeping.

Immediately Judith got up and held Vijay by the shoulders and said, "Hold yourself Papa. All your life you have been counseling couples to do the same. Now it's your turn. Don't forget, you must practice what you preach."

"Yes my darling Judy, you're right. But I never expected all these things to befall me one after another and in quick succession. Finally I too am made of flesh and blood… with emotions."

"Yes Papa, you have begun second chapter of your life and all of us are supporting you for your decision. We are always with you, Papa."

"I decided to go to Melbourne because all these things in the house: the bed, her closets full of saris and dresses, the comfort-room, the kitchen, the utensils, the broom, the vacuum, the dining table and even the doormats started to haunt me. I was on the verge of getting deranged. My going to Melbourne was timely and we must thank God for sending Jasmine in the nick of time in my life."

The D'Souza clan in Melbourne was extremely excited about the new arrival in the family at any time. Jasmine was admitted to the Birth Centre of Angliss Hospital.

Contractions… false alarm… contractions… false alarm…the sequence repeated. Finally the bag burst and Vijay was taken into the Delivery Room.

This was the first time Vijay was going to witness childbirth, despite having two children already. At that time in India father was strictly prohibited from witnessing his own wife delivering a child.

Vijay had been instructed and rehearsed about the routine of delivery procedure with a female rubber dummy. So at this time he was ready with head-cap, green apron, gloves and he fully sterilized, ready to enter Laminar Flow conditioned DR.

As the labour pain started, Jasmine started to huff-puff and scream intermittently. Vijay felt sorry for Jasmine and stroked her forehead. Pressure on the cervix and contractions of the muscles of the uterus caused Jasmine terrible pain. With strong cramping in the abdomen, groin and the back, the pain also went to hips and down the thighs as well. Vijay helped Jasmine with the breathing apparatus every now and then.

After about ten minutes of labour there appeared a small head with pitch black bushy hair and within minutes she was relieved of the bundle of flesh, but with a life-line attached. Wow! Vijay was amazed to witness the miracle of unfolding of human life.

There was a loud welcome cry of the baby. The midwife cut the navel chord and clamped it. Wiping the babe with soft cloth she placed it on Jasmine's chest. Vijay bent and kissed Jasmine's forehead saying, "Lovely darling, you made it! Both of you are safe."

"And…you…too…honey…" Jasmine blabbered.

After a while the Midwife wrapped the baby with warm piece of cloth and gave it in father's hands. Vijay was overwhelmed to see their daughter and shouted spontaneously, "Maria…my Maria…is back!"

*****

After two days Jasmine was discharged from the Angliss Hospital. Sanjay already had a baby seat bucket in his car. A new member to 202, Ross Street was being added. From this abode, 'Maria II', would carry on the legacy of Himmat Singh and Jessica Smith into the future. Of course on playful shoulders of parents Vijay and Jasmine!

It was an exhilarating view to watch when the entourage approached 202, Ross Street. Magpie sitting on the wooden railing and holding a flower stem in his beak, welcomed the new-born babe –Maria Jr. being carried by loving parents Vijay and Jasmine.

The Magpie produced a welcome song with his usual sub-song rattles and grating coos–meaning:

"Wow, what a beautiful baby with blue eyes,

Curved eye-brows and curly black hair!

A blend of Indo-Australian inheritance,

With integrated culture a hybrid heir!"

Epilogue

Maria junior began growing up in an excellent Indo-Australian cultural blend with abundant love and care by Jasmine, Vijay and Jessica; and of course uncle Sanjay, Aunt Nilufer and cousin Ajay. She had Barbie-doll looks with dark curly hair, laced with a few golden-blond streaks just above her forehead going back towards both ears. During East Indian Community gatherings Maria Jr. became the centre of attraction, as children gathered and played around her.

Emigrants from Indian sub-continent during the past 70/80 or so years have grown to a sizable number. Like immigrants of other nationalities, Indians too while enjoying civic amenities, shoulder their responsibilities towards Australia's economic and cultural growth and have become integral part of Australian ethos.

Of course from time to time there are untoward incidents among people of various nationalities, ethnicity and religions, from which today no country in the world is exempt. For their survival, Media only highlights one bad event and remains silent about the nine good ones.

But that's life...without challenges life would be monotonous and uninteresting. That is how Melbourne Magpie looks at Vijay's and Jasmine's struggles, awarded with fulfilment and happiness.